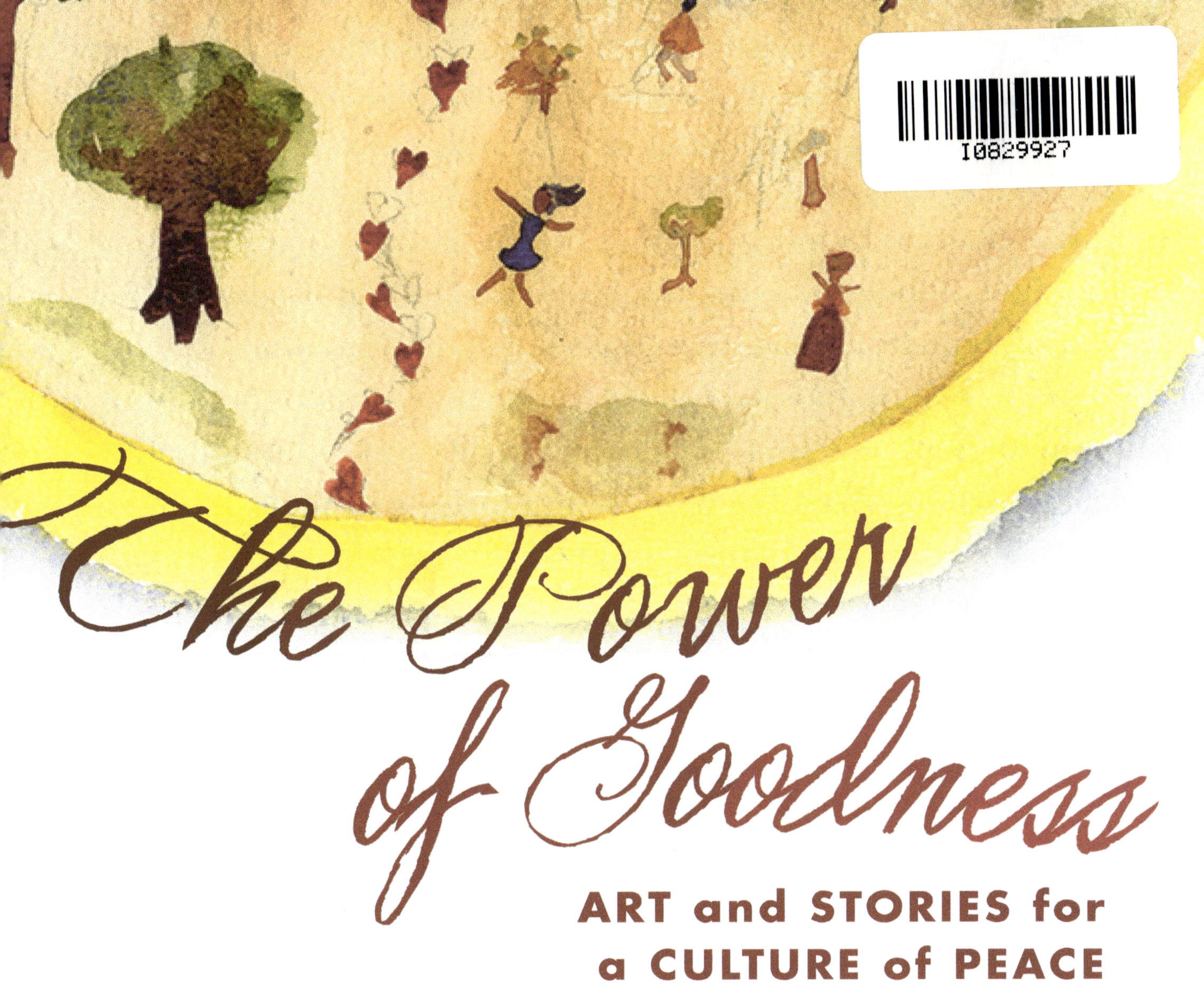

The Power of Goodness

ART and STORIES for a CULTURE of PEACE and JUSTICE

SECOND EDITION

stories selected and authored for Ukrainian and Chechen children and children everywhere

Edited by
Nadine Hoover

This book accompanies **The Power of Goodness Art Exhibition**, a traveling exhibition of original artwork by children ages 6-19, see FriendsPeaceTeams.org/Power-of-Goodness.

Friends Peace Teams is a nonprofit organization registered in the United States supporting peace and justice ministries around the world dedicated to collecting true stories of the Power of Goodness and offering Alternatives to Violence Project mini-workshops to spread the message of peace, nonviolence, and reconciliation to young people and adults.

Peacebuilding UK is a charitable organization in the UK dedicated to using Power of Goodness stories to train teachers, school counselors, and psychologists around the world to support young people surviving war and violence.

Accepting tax-deductible donations in Australia, UK, and USA, see: FriendsPeaceTeam.org, memo: Power of Goodness. The book is available at CourageousGifts.com.

The Power of Goodness grew out of a story collection by Philadelphia Yearly Meeting (Quakers) that later became *Lighting Candles in the Dark* (FGC, 2001) available at QuakerBooks.org.

Foreword by Pete Seeger
Edited by Nadine Hoover
    The Power of Goodness: Art and Stories for a Culture of Peace and Justice, Second Edition

ISBN 978-1-7356337-4-9

1. Peace & Nonviolence
2. World History
3. Art Exhibition Catalog - Group Show

Cover Art:	Maggie MacArthur-McKay
Cover Design:	Terese Longva
Curatorial Advisor:	Dawn Bennett
Technical Support:	Devin Henry

"I expect to pass through

this world but once;

any good thing therefore I can do,

or any kindness that I can show

to any fellow creature,

let me do it now;

let me not defer or neglect it,

for I shall not pass this way again."

~ Stephen Grellet, Quaker c. 1800

In these dangerous times we can all be encouraged to be active by reading this book.

Hooray for all the people, young and old, in widely separated parts of the world, who have cooperated to put it together.

If we all get active in some little way, we will see this power leap over barriers of language, barriers of religion, barriers of politics.

I'll give you an anonymous poem taken from the writings of philosopher William James, from a little over a hundred years ago:

> I am done
>
> with great things and big things
>
> great institutions and big success
>
> and I am for
>
> those tiny, invisible, molecular moral forces
>
> that work from individual to individual
>
> through the crannies of the world
>
> like so many rootlets
>
> or like the capillary oozing of water
>
> yet which, if you give them time
>
> will rend
>
> the hardest monuments of man's pride.

Pete Seeger

Table of Contents

Table of Contents

Traveling Art Exhibitions

This English-language version of *The Power of Goodness* (2nd Ed, 2023) was published to accompany the Power of Goodness Art Exhibition of original children's artwork, available in the United States.

The four sections of the book represent the four exhibits, each with an introductory panel, seven to nine story panels, and 23-25 original artworks available for display:

- *Seeking Justice Together* (children and adults)
- *Healing Ourselves and the Earth* (children and adults)
- *Reaching Out to Each Other* (for older children and adults)
- *Love & Hope* (for younger children and adults)

The art show is a fundraiser for the interactive events offered to children living in violent, impoverished circumstances around the world. We accept donations to spread these stories and workshops in the world. *The Power of Goodness* stories, children's art exhibition, community events, and classroom instruction are our contribution to a global culture of peace and justice.

We invite you to volunteer, send your stories or feedback, make a tax-deductible donation, or book an art exhibition. Donate in Australia, Europe, or the United States at FriendsPeaceTeams.org, or donate to PeacebuildingUK.org. *Thank you!*

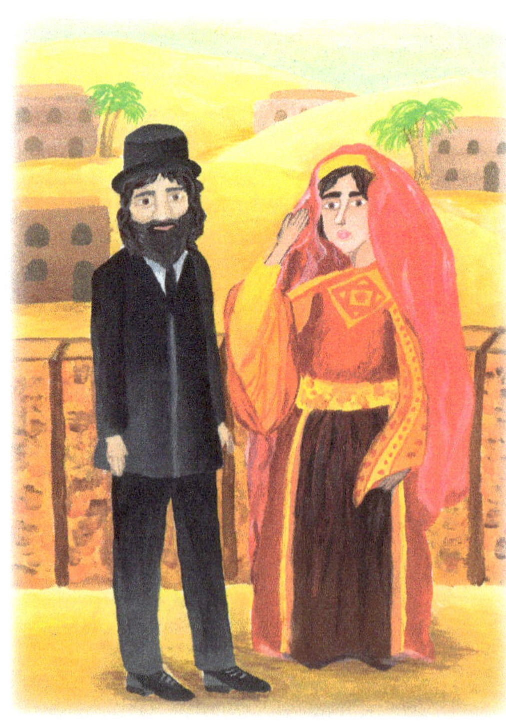

Anna Nikolaychuk, age 15, A3 tempera

Preface

Wherever there is war, there are children. Children need stories of peace and justice, especially when all they have known is war. *The Power of Goodness* shares true stories from around the world.

The stories depict the power of loving kindness in action. Friendship, forgiveness, and reconciliation emerge where paths of fairness and integrity are unclear. A deep respect for the dignity of self, others, and nature emboldens people. Readers experience the joy of seeing from so many perspectives.

To help children overcome the war fervor after WWII, Quakers collected practical examples of how real people lived their faith in peace, nonviolence, and justice. Philadelphia Yearly Meeting (PYM) of the Religious Society of Friends (Quakers) published this anthology of stories titled *Candles in the Dark* (PYM, 1964). Later, it was published as *Lighting Candles in the Dark: Stories of Courage and Love in Action* by Friends General Conference (1992, reprinted 2001).

Engaged in movements for peace, women's rights, civil rights, and alternative education, Quakers created the Children's Creative Response to Violence (CCRC, 1972) and Alternatives to Violence Project (AVP, 1975) workshops. Children and adults practice nonviolence skills in these interactive workshops. Power of Goodness later drew on this interactive approach to explore the meaning of these stories in classrooms and workshops.

Russian and US Quakers formed the Quaker US\USSR Committee in 1985 to build friendships after long isolation. It became known as the Quaker FSU Committee after the Soviet Union dissolved in 1991. Janet Riley took copies of *Lighting Candles in the Dark* to Novgorod, Russia in 1994 to teach English as a second language.

These stories inspired pre-teens and teachers, who said: *There are moments in these stories where we can do the same. They teach us how to act. Yes, they teach us to be kind and to help one another. They show us another way. They show that love is important. It's good for us to know about children in other places in the world. They give us ideas for our lives.* So they translated the stories into Russian.

In March 1995, during the Chechen War, Mothers of Russian Soldiers, Buddhists, and Quakers organized a peace march from Moscow to Grozny. Stories from Chechen women moved Janet Riley and other Friends in Moscow to gather stories from Russia and Chechnya.

Mikhail Roshchin and Chris Hunter brought boxes of the Russian *Lighting Candles in the Dark* to Hawa Mahmudova. She used them in children's art classes in a basement in Grozny, the capitol of Chechnya. As war raged around them, young Chechens, six to nineteen years old, created powerful illustrations for selected stories from *Lighting Candles in the Dark* and their local own stories. A trilingual edition of *The Power of Goodness* (Friends International Library, 2005) in Russian, Chechen, and English was printed. With the support of the US Institute for Peace, they printed over 10,000 copies.

Chris Hunter of Peacebuilding UK found support for Chechen psychologists from Little Star to use the stories with children. Janet Riley worked with teachers to develop discussion questions for a teachers' manual that Little Star could use with teachers and school counselors. They added activities and games related to each story for children to gain skills for their psycho-social well-being.

Venera Minazova said that when her children faced difficulties, they often ask: "Do any stories in that book have similar problems? What did they do?"

Hundreds of thousands of Chechen children have read the stories and done the activities. Hundreds of teachers from primary school through college use the stories and activities in their classroom. A former Chechen Minister of Education (2007) declared that "*The Power of Goodness* is a gift to Chechnya's children."

In 2012, Friends International Library transferred Power of Goodness to Friends Peace Teams and Peacebuilding UK. The Little Star psychologists trained Ukrainians who were seeking therapeutic supports following the 2014 Russian occupation of Eastern Ukraine. Teachers, counselors, and aid workers throughout Ukraine found the activities healing, and felt they brought hope to Ukrainian children and families.

In 2018, Nadine Hoover brought the Alternatives to Violence Project workshop series, Creating Cultures of Peace, to the Power of Goodness facilitators. This expanded their understandings and activities in line with the focus of the stories on nonviolence and reconciliation. The first set of the activities focus on personal transformation. They cover sharing power, becoming resilient, and learning through play. The second set of activities focus on social transformation. They cover overcoming oppression and discerning a consensus of conscience.

A Ukrainian participant at the 2015 training in Odesa described: "We watched the news of the Russian invasion in Chechnya, Georgia, and then Crimea, as if it were a TV show. We didn't imagine the war could come here." Participants remarked: *Thank you so much for coming to be with us and not forget us. These stories remind us of the strengths we have that we can use in our daily lives. Simple acts can be the most powerful.*

Ukrainians collected their own stories and organized young people to illustrate them. With the support of Caritas, they printed a trilingual Ukrainian edition (2022) in Ukrainian, Russian, and English.

Through Friends Peace Teams, these stories along with the interactive activities spread from Chechnya and Ukraine to Indonesia, Jeju Island, Philippines, and West Papua. Peace workers in Africa and Latin America are showing interest. Young people and adults appreciate the stories as they struggle to keep their humanity in the face of ongoing militarism, war, and violence. Both the stories and artwork help children in areas of armed conflict to heal from their experiences and stay resilient.

Power of Goodness now offers 1-2 hour events organized around a theme and a story using Alternatives to Violence Project (AVP) session format and interactive activities. These events bring the stories alive through interactions among people sharing their own experiences.

Facilitators do events with people of any age around the world—street children, refugee camps, war zones, former war zones, impoverished communities, and others suffering from exploitation, racism, and violence. These stories, especially when adding discussions and skill-building activities, bring fresh hope and courage to people crying for peace and justice for themselves and their children.

As militarism, war, and violence continue, so must our efforts to bring the lessons of peace and justice to those in its wake, especially children. We hope this book and its accompanying art exhibition, learning activities, and training sessions convey our faith. Across religion, class and culture, we share a faith in the power of the Living Spirit to give life, joy, peace and prosperity through love, integrity and compassionate justice among people who live in simplicity, equality, and nonviolence. We make no enemies, take no sides. Rather, we seek to raise up new generations in the liberty and joy that we experience when we live in accord with love and conscience. We call everyone on this small, tender planet to work together for a peaceful, just future.

Acknowledgements

We extend our gratitude to generations of people, as well as to the authors and illustrators who donated their works to support peaceful, just lives for us all. Quakers after WWII collected stories of nonviolence and reconciliation; Janet Riley Moles shared those stories. Johan Maurer, Mikhail Roshchin, Sylvia Mangalam, and Chris Hunter of the Friends International Library printed the Russian version to share the practical and spiritual Quaker message of peace.

Friends House Moscow and Moscow Friends Meeting offered tremendous support as Mikhail Roshchin and Musa Akhmadov gathered Chechen and Russian stories. Translators applied great care and skill to offer valid and vivid translations: Tatiana Pavlova, John Coutts, Polina Sparks, Said-Hamzat Nunuev, Hasan Turkayev, Said-Usman Yahiev, Shukran Suleimanova, and Denis Smetanin in Russian and Chechen; Subhash Chandra and Ram Paudel in Nepali; Nanik and Ratih Puspito Rini in Indonesia; Melanie Siaw in Malay; and Charles Rand in Spanish.

Hawa Mahmudova supported Chechen young people to produce compelling artwork under difficult circumstances. Peacebuilding-UK, the Centre for Peacebuilding and Community Development, the Little Star psychologists, and the Chechen children, teachers, and counselors brought this work alive.

Lena Melnik, the Odesa Mediation Group, and a network of Ukrainian psychologists used the book throughout Ukraine and collected new Ukrainian stories, and provided translations of existing stories.

We are grateful for support of the United States Institute of Peace (USIP), Institute for Foreign Cultural Relations, the German Federal Foreign Office, and the Religious Society of Friends (Quakers): Chace Fund Committee, Obadiah Brown Benevolent Fund, Jonathan E. Rhoads Trust, Sara Bowers Fund,

Community Agreements

People-to-people friendships weave the fabric of peace, yet some of the worst violence in the world occurs among loved ones and neighbors. To preserve peace and establish justice, we commit to practicing, in both private and public life, this set of Community Agreements.

Community Agreements

- *Affirm self and others; no put-downs or put ups.*
- *Stop, listen, don't interrupt.*
- *Speak simply & truthfully, without fear of mistakes.*
- *Speak from your own experience, not others' without permission.*
- *Make friends not enemies with people similar to and different from yourself.*
- *Ask for and offer hospitality, feedback, and help.*
- *Tend emotion, then speak directly if in dispute.*
- *Use what's needed and share the rest fairly.*
- *Use your rights to pass and to consultation.*
- *Volunteer yourself only, not others.*
- *Care for self, group, community and nature.*
- *Live in integrity with life's transforming power.*

We each practice these agreements, speak up when one is violated, remind each other, and discuss ways to apply them to create regenerative cultures of peace and justice.

International Outreach Committee, Pemberton Fund, Shoemaker Fund, Sandy Spring Friends Meeting, New York Yearly Meeting; as well as Daniel C. Shaffer, Cynthia and Miles Edwards, Kingdon Duane, Asta Hamann, Mary Deni Foster, Kim and Mark Tsocanos, and others. The quality of the art exhibition and this book is due to the enthusiasm and expertise of Dawn Bennett, Scott Alario, Jessen Case, Emily Guth, Devin Henry, Marguerite Keyes, and Amanda Micek.

Part 1: Seeking Justice Together

Stories from Chechnya, Israel, Palestine, Russia, and USA

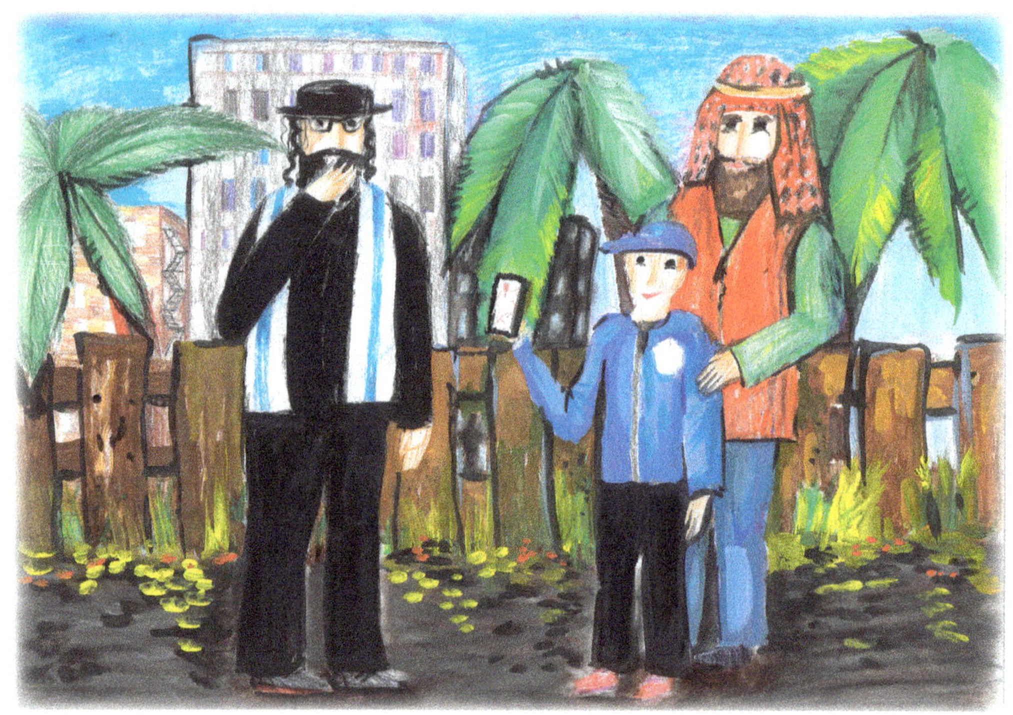

Andrij Veremchuk, age 14, A3 tempera

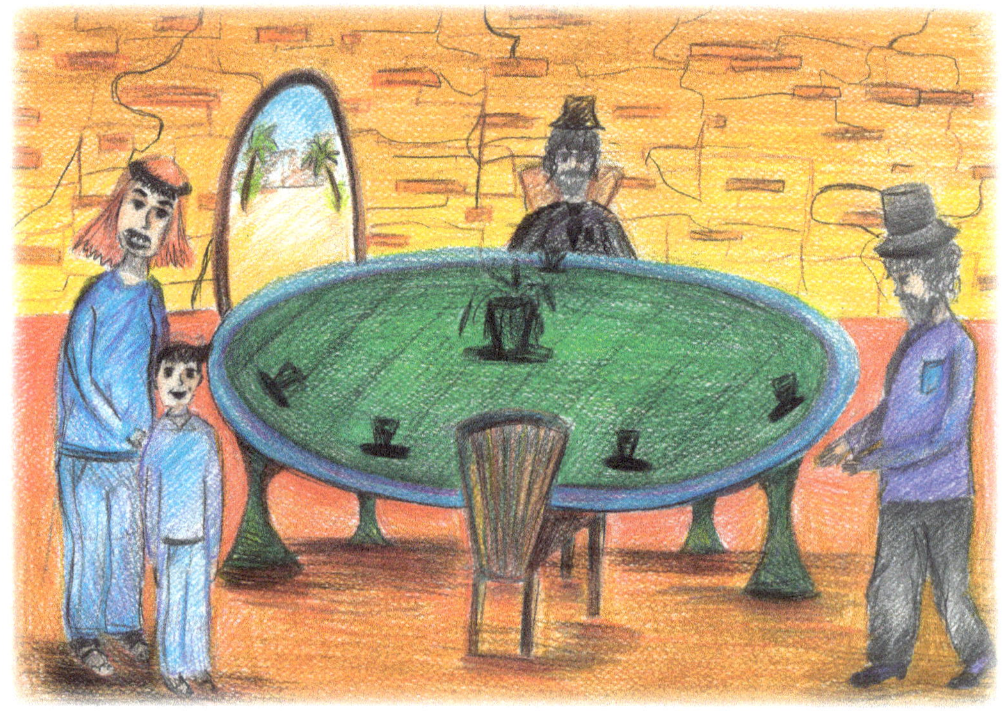

Andrij Duma, age 15, A3 chalk

Across the Fence

by Hanan Schlesinger, Israel

It was a miracle that we ever met at all.

I had lived in Israel for 35 years, but didn't really know any Palestinians when, a few years ago, I received a visitor to my home. He offered me an opportunity to meet neighbors who had been unknown and invisible to me. I could go to a meeting a 20 minute walk from my home in the West Bank. I told my wife, "I'm going to meet some Palestinians."

"Don't go," she cried, "it's too dangerous!"

I feared she was right, but went anyway. Walking through Palestinian vineyards and fields, I could feel my heart pounding. When I arrived, I was stunned. Twenty Israelis and twenty Palestinians were standing and sitting in small circles, talking and eating, together. In thirty-five years in Gush Etzion, I had never seen anything like it.

I saw a Palestinian woman dressed in brown, from head to toe, standing alone. I greeted her. We both marveled, "I can't believe I'm talking with you."

"I know," she replied, "I can't believe I'm talking with you either." She called her son, Yazin. He was wearing a windbreaker with Seeds of Peace on his jacket. I reeled again as the voice in my mind said, "Palestinians don't know the word peace…"

Abruptly, I asked out loud, "What is Seeds of Peace?"

Yazin explained that it was a camp in Maine, in the United States, that brings Palestinian and Israeli young people together to meet each other. Here was a Palestinian teenager explaining to me, the Rabbi, the ideas and practices of peace and reconciliation!

She then introduced Jamal, her husband. They lived in Beit Ummar, a neighboring village, very close and yet so far away. I heard a voice in my mind say, "That's where terrorists come from–blood thirsty people, who throw rocks and want to kill us." I also heard how my wife say, "Go to Beit Ummar!" in frustration, meaning "Go to hell!"

As I caught my breath, Jamal took out a smartphone. I reeled again; smartphones were quite new at the time, yet Palestinians have smartphones? Jamal opened Google Maps; I'd never seen Google Maps. Jamal pointed out his house. It was directly across the fence from mine! Jamal and I were literally neighbors, with an impermeable fence between us.

Out of nowhere Jamal said, "When my kids see people like you, with yarmulkes (Jewish head coverings) and long beards, they cry."

Jolted from my thoughts, I asked, "Why? What's so scary about yarmulkes and beards?"

He caught his breath, surprised and confused. It seemed all too obvious, "Well… because people with yarmulkes and beards carry submachine guns and kill our kids!" It took a minute to sink in. It was like looking at myself in a mirror, seeing how Jamal and his children saw me. Jewish people liked to go outside the fence to walk in the land of the biblical stories where Abraham, Isaac, and Jacob had walked. But of course we carried submachine guns when we went, to protect ourselves, because it was dangerous.

"You know, Jamal, we carry guns because we're afraid of you," I told him.

"No," he replied, "It is we who are afraid of you."

My mind was racing. I wondered why we had so much fear of each other. Was it because we lived so close together, Palestinian and Israeli, but had no contact? We lived in different areas, worshipped in different ways in different buildings, had different media, newspapers, radio and television, in different languages, so we got different news, and therefore we really did live in different worlds, with different understandings, and different realities just across the fence.

But as I saw these faces of human beings and listened to their stories, we weren't that different.

I was not sure what happened to me that evening, but whatever it was, it changed me forever.

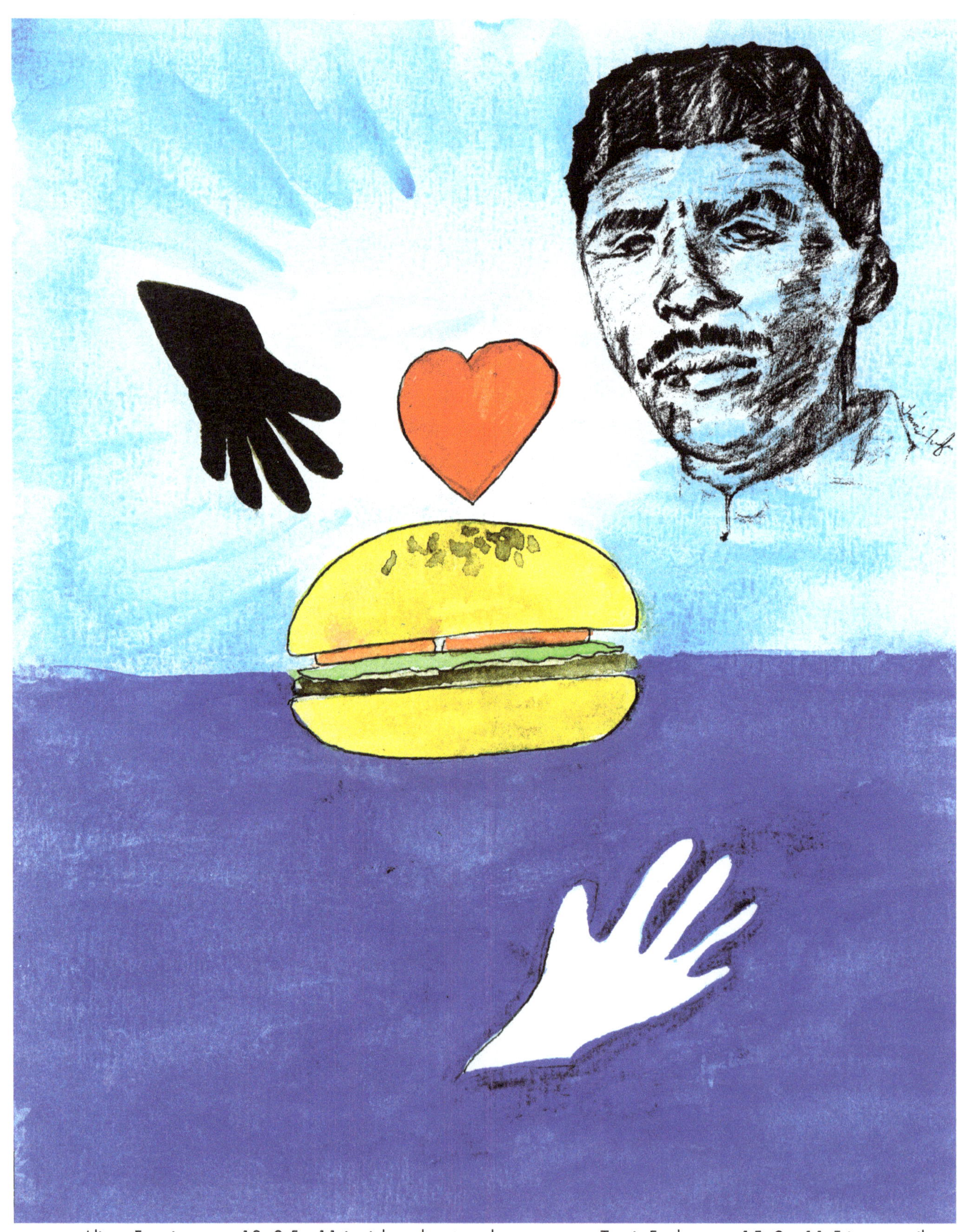

Alison Fanning, age 13, 8.5 x 11 in. ink and watercolor   Travis Fugler, age 15, 9 x 11.5 inc. pencil

Experiment in Fairness

by Bayard Rustin, United States of America

Bayard Rustin was an African American leader who worked for equal rights for all in North America through the Fellowship of Reconciliation (FOR) in the 1940s and 1950s, then later through the civil rights movement.

Between speaking engagements in a Midwestern college town I went into a small restaurant to buy a hamburger and a glass of milk. I had not been sitting in the restaurant long before I noticed I was being ignored.

After waiting about 10 minutes I decided that the conflict had to be faced. I moved to stand directly before a waitress so she could not overlook me and said, "I would like to have a hamburger."

"I'm sorry," she replied, "but we can't serve . . . er . . . er . . . you, er . . . colored people here."

"Who's responsible for this?" I asked.

She made her reply in two gestures – the first indicating a woman standing in the rear; and the second, a finger to the lip, an obvious appeal for me not to involve her in any way.

I walked directly to the woman standing near the coffee in the rear of the restaurant.

"I would like to know why it is impossible for me to be served here."

"Well . . . er . . ." she stuttered. "It's . . . it's because we don't do that in this town. They don't serve colored people in any of the restaurants."

"Okay, but why? Do you believe that doing so would upset your customers?"

I then appealed to her to make an experiment in the extension of democracy.

After some hesitation she agreed to the following terms: I would sit in the front of the restaurant for ten minutes, during which time I would not eat my hamburger. We would count the number of people who left or did not come in because of me. If we saw one such person, I would leave.

If we did not, I could eat my hamburger.

I waited 15 minutes. Then she approached me, picked up the cold hamburger, placed a hot one before me, and said simply, "What will you have to drink with it?"

I have been given to understand that Mrs. Duffy continues to serve everyone without embarrassment or conflict, which is indeed a courageous thing in these circumstances.

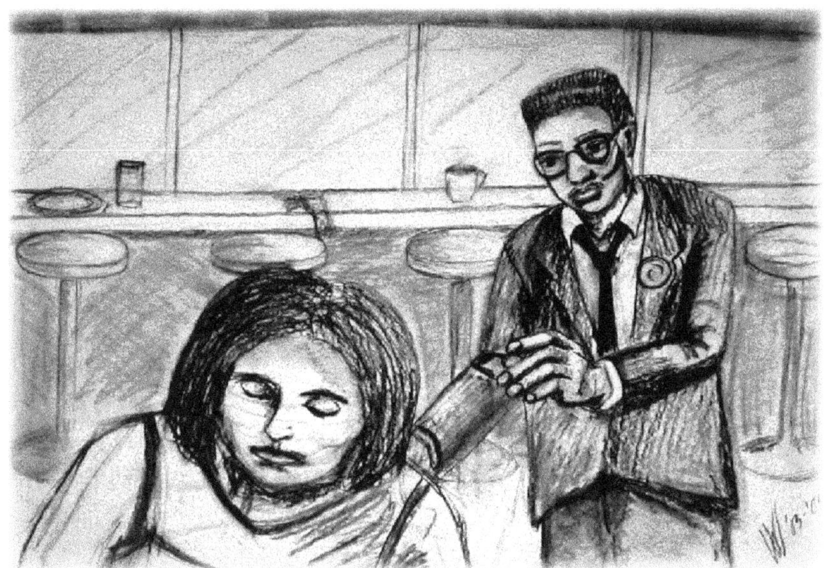

Valerie White, 11 x 7.5 in. pencil

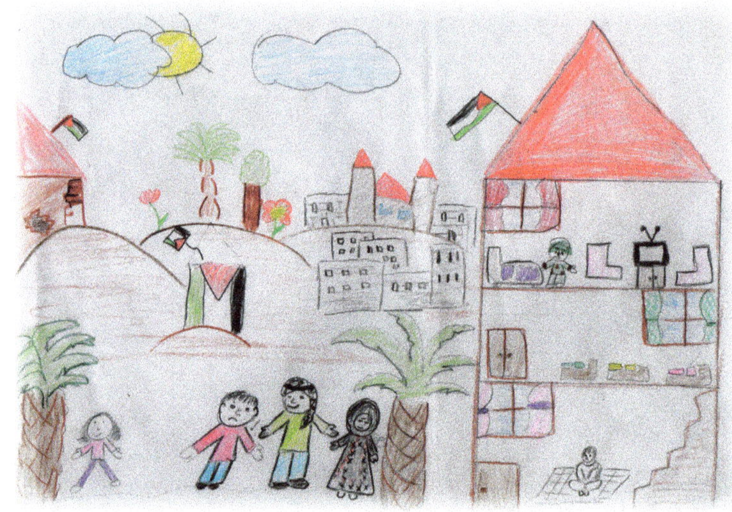

Coneen Hanna,
13 x 9.5 in.
colored pencil

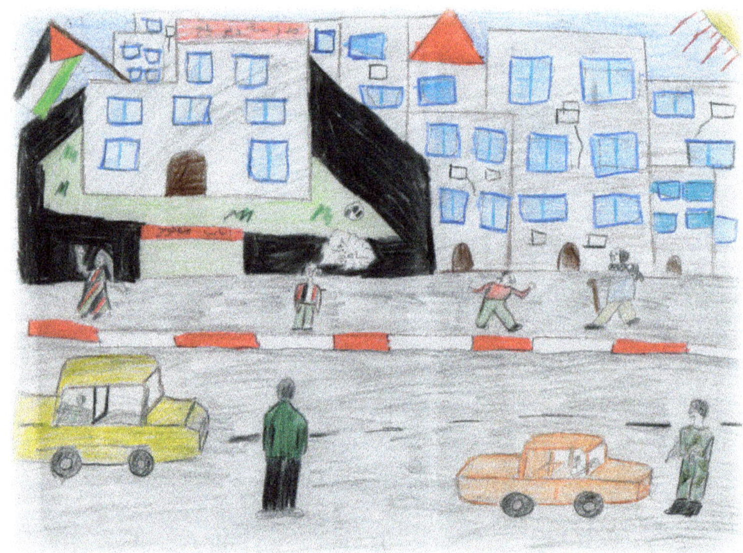

George Siniora,
13 x 9.5 in.
colored pencil

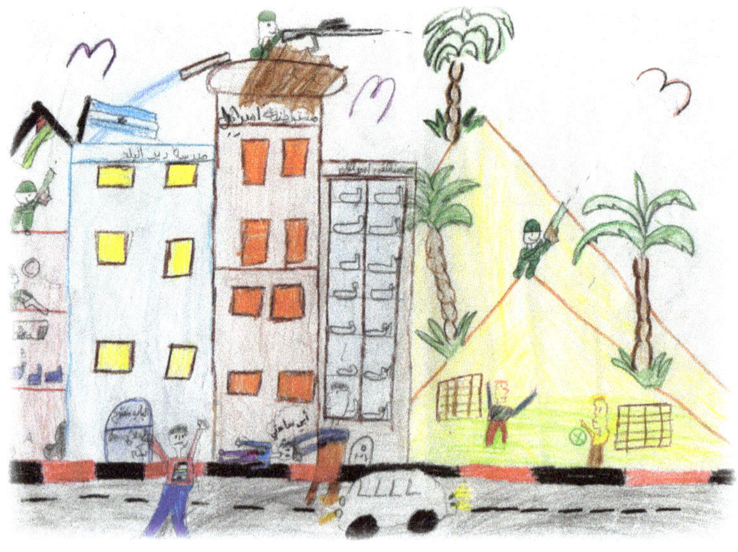

Ahmad Badran,
13.5 x 10 in.
colored pencil

To Forgive is Divine

a story of Yousef Bashir as told by Anthony Manousos, Palestine

As a Palestinian, I grew up in Deir el-Balah in Gaza with my family, beside the Israeli settlement Kfar Darom. I didn't notice politics or poverty. I played sports, dreaming of becoming a soccer star.

But one day in 2000, Israeli soldiers with M-16s told us to leave our home. We asked, "Why? We've done nothing wrong!" Mother wanted to leave at once with our neighbors. But father said, "I will stay, no matter what, to keep the family home."

Israeli soldiers moved into the second and third floors they called "Area C," only Israeli military allowed. They covered our roof with camouflage nets, barbed wire, and guns. The living room, where seven of had to stay at night, was "Area A," where Palestinians had power, but we called it jail. The kitchen, bathroom, and bedrooms were "Area B," where Palestinians could go but Israelis controlled security. We had to ask permission to go to the kitchen, and a soldier came with us to the bathroom.

How we survived this for five years I don't know. Maybe through love of home, maybe our belief that everyone is human. My father said, "Both Palestinians and Israelis are Abraham's children and have the right to peace." But I was not so sure.

I was waving goodbye to visiting UN workers when I felt something enter my back. It felt strange. It didn't hurt at first. I crumpled to the ground. My father took me in his arms. Then the pain hit so intense that I whispered the Shahadat, words Muslims say when we die.

But my father said, "You will not die." That's how he is. He never gives up.

I passed out. I woke in a Palestinian hospital with an I.V. My father smiled. He told me they shot me in the back, and that the bullet was in my spine so it was too dangerous to operate. "But you'll be okay," he said.

I was 15 and couldn't move my legs. I asked, "Will I be able to walk?"

My father said, "If God wills. The doctors are doing everything they can." I became so depressed I stopped talking.

Then I went to a new hospital where the nurses and doctors spoke Hebrew! My dad was with an Israeli nurse who spoke in a kind voice like my mother's. It was the first time an Israeli smiled at me, or I saw a civilian Israeli. Over the next few months, the doctors and nurses who visited me smiled, joked, and were kind. Could Israelis truly be human? When my parents returned to Gaza, I missed them and was nervous about being alone.

At first, the Israeli family of my roommate didn't like being with me. But when they heard my story and saw I was lonely, they were kind. They brought me gifts and made sure I had what I needed. While I struggled to regain my health, I had lengthy conversations with my father on why so many people get hurt and die, and whether forgiveness is possible. Slowly my attitude changed. One Israeli soldier shot me, but many Israelis saved my life. What my parents said was true. Israelis are human, and I felt truly human too. I wanted to make the world more peaceful.

Doctors could not remove the bullet from my back, but I walk fine now. And I got my chance to be a peacemaker. I spent a summer at Seeds of Peace in the U.S., a camp where Israeli and Palestinian teens talk to each other and make friends. Afterward, I no longer wanted to take sides. My family and friends rejected me as a traitor, but my parents always supported me. I knew that "to err is human, to forgive divine."

An Israeli soldier stationed in my home became interested in my story. I told him I wanted to be a peacemaker. I suggested he become a Seeds of Peace counsellor and gave him a Seeds of Peace T-shirt. He smiled and said he would wear it when his military service was done.

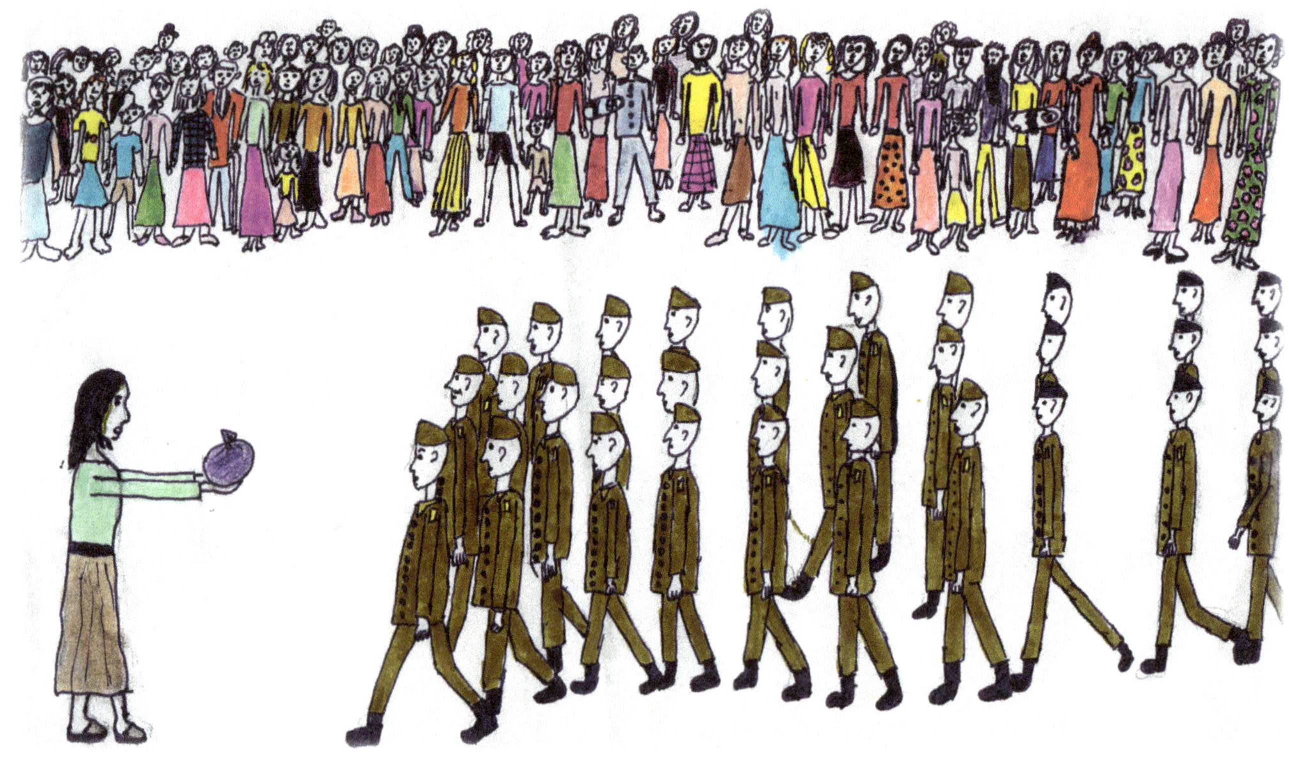

Unknown, 7.5 x 11.5 in. felt-tip pen and watercolor

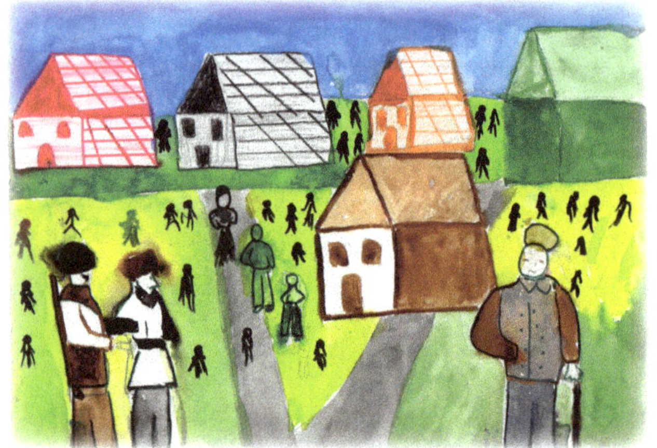

Unknown, 11.5 x 8 in. felt-tip pen and watercolor

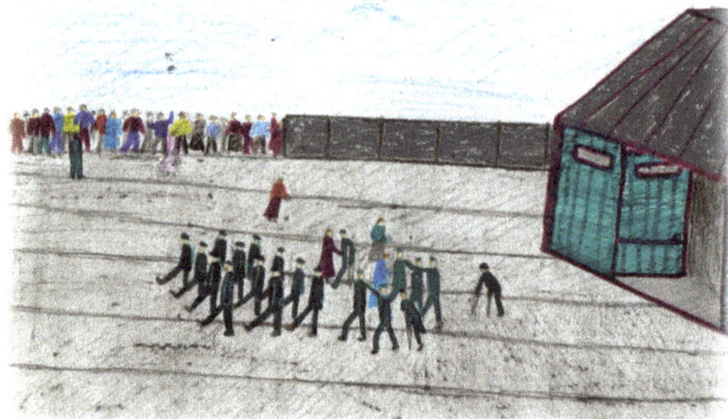

Unknown, 12 x 8.5 in. pencil, felt-tip pen and oil pastel

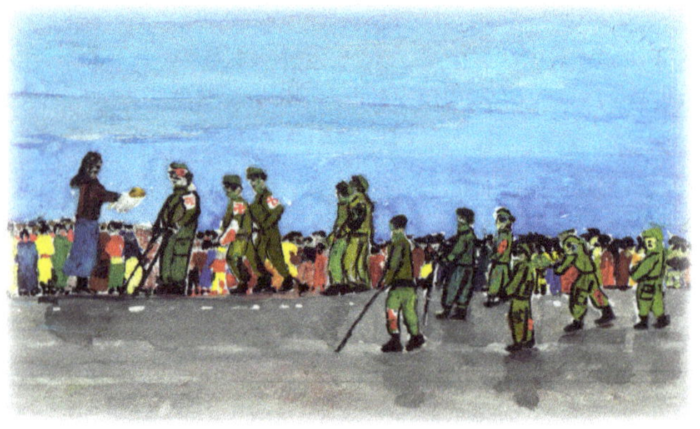

Unknown, lost original, felt-tip pen and watercolor

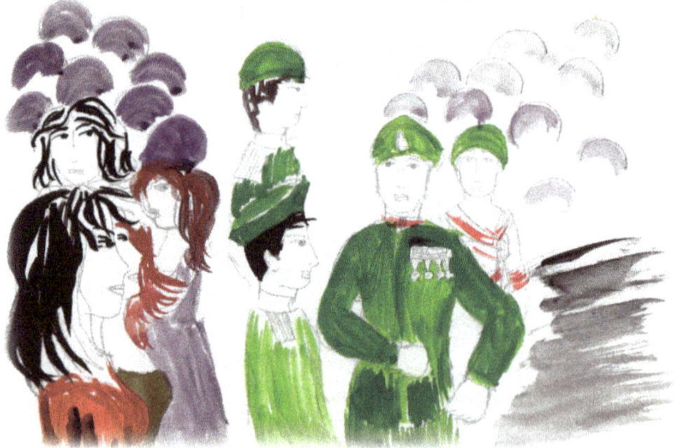

Unknown, 11.75 x 8.25 in. pencil and watercolor

Mercy: A Poet's Memory

by Yevgeny Yevtushenko, Russia

In 1944 Mama and I returned to Moscow.

And for the first time I saw our enemies. About twenty thousand German prisoners – if I have the numbers correct – were to pass through the streets of Moscow in a single column.

The sidewalks were crowded with people. The soldiers and police could hardly hold them back.

They were mostly women – Russian women with hands rough from hard work, lips unaccustomed to lipstick, and thin stooped shoulders that had borne the brunt of the war. Every one of them must have had a father or a husband, a brother or a son killed by the Germans.

The women gazed in hatred at the spot where the column of German prisoners was due to appear.

There it was at last.

First came the generals, sticking their arrogant chins out, pressing their scornful lips together, everything about them aiming to show superiority over their lowly victors.

"They smell of deodorant, the bastards," said someone in the crowd.

The women clenched their fists. The soldiers and policemen battled to hold them back.

And suddenly something happened to the crowd.

The people saw a column of German soldiers, emaciated, unshaven, all in pitiful rags and filthy, bloodstained bandages. Leaning on their comrades' shoulders or on crutches, they walked with their heads bowed low.

The street fell silent; the only thing you could hear was shuffling boots and creaking crutches.

All at once I saw an elderly woman in tattered boots lay her hand on a policeman's shoulder. "Let me through," she said.

There must have been something about her that made him step aside.

The woman went up to the column of Germans, took something wrapped in a kerchief from inside her coat, and unfolded it. It was the heel of a loaf of black bread.

And suddenly women started running up to the soldiers from all sides, shoving bread, cigarettes, anything, into their hands.

They were enemies no longer. They were people.

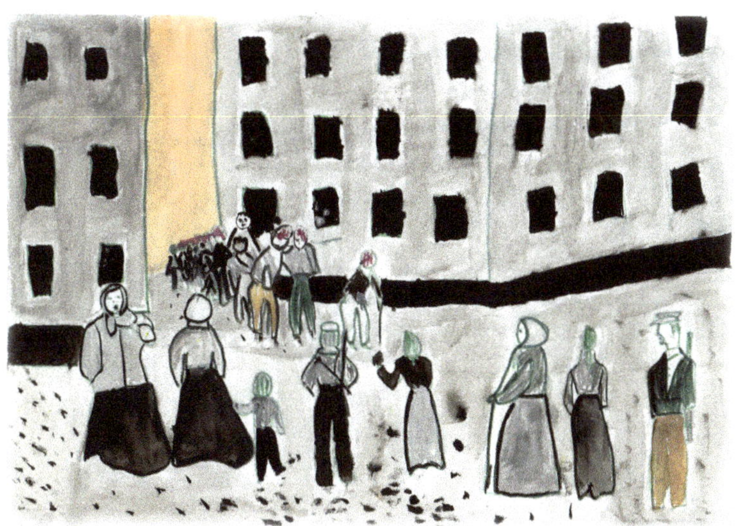

Unknown, 11.5 x 8 in. felt-tip pen and watercolor

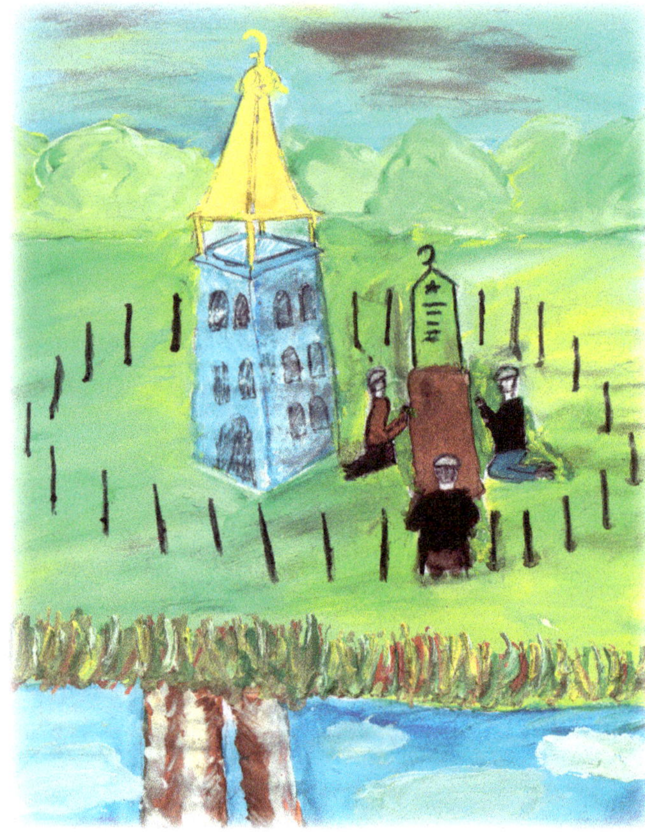

Rovzan Elnukayeva, 8 x 11.5 in. watercolor

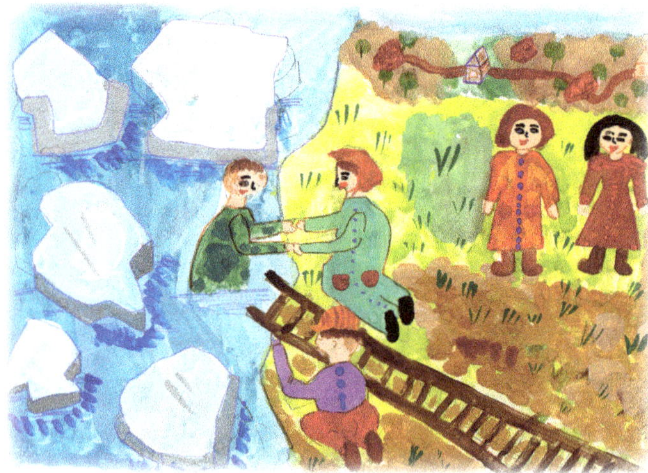

Lera Nevsorova, age 8, 16.5 x 11.75 in. tempera

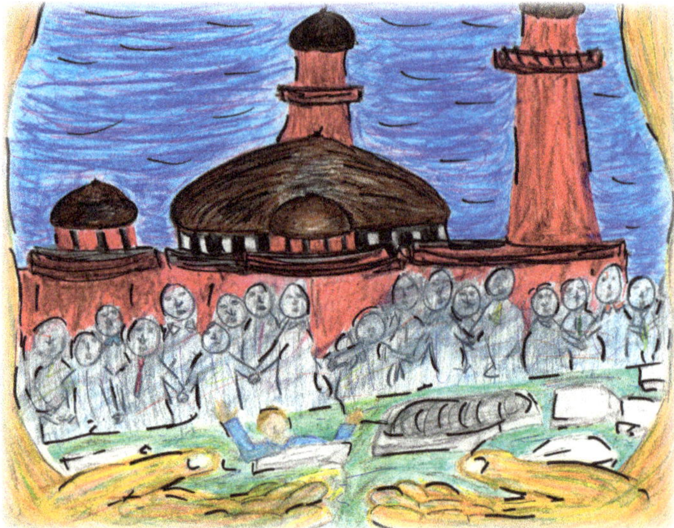

Heather Kroger, age 20,13.25 x 10.25 in.
ink and colored pencil

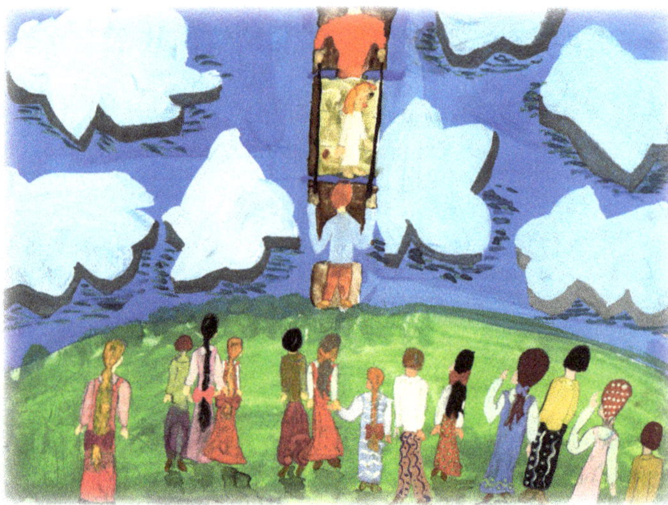

Alyona Ovdenko, age 8, 16.5 x 11.75 in. tempera

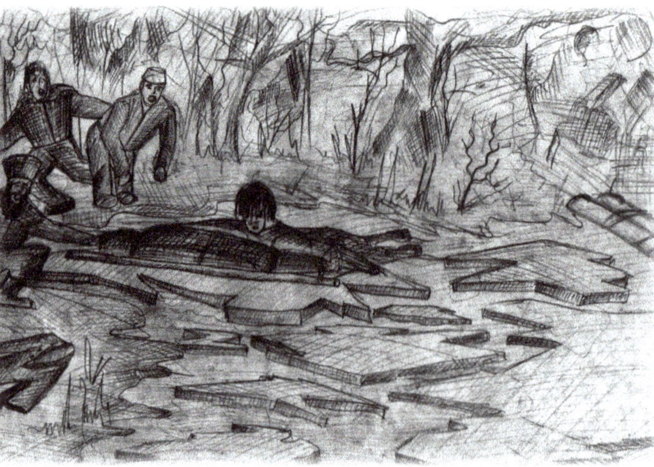

Artur Ymarov, age 14, 11 x 8.5 in. pencil

The Mosque

by German Kuznetsov-Valin, Russia

One day my friend and I were caught in a cloudburst. His friend Akhmet welcomed us and let us dry out in his house. Inside was a large, expensively framed color photograph.

"Do you like it?" asked Akhmet. "It's the Rashida Mosque. There are two very interesting stories about it."

The first happened long ago.

Ismail, a blacksmith, was known far and wide because he could make anything and never turned down any request.

One day he was found dead; his heart had failed. Everyone came to the funeral, in a long procession toward the cemetery across the river. The river was in flood; ice and water from the mountains washed out its bridges and rushed over rocky rapids.

Men struggled to build a bridge, but it looked dangerous.

The body was tied to the bier. Men pulled the bier across the bridge with a rope, but halfway across the rope escaped them. The bier slid onto a sheet of ice, which the current carried toward rapids just downstream.

People ran along the bank, shouting. A young Russian soldier heard the Tartars' cries and leapt into the water. Ice-sheets knocked him off his feet. The current dragged him toward the rapids.

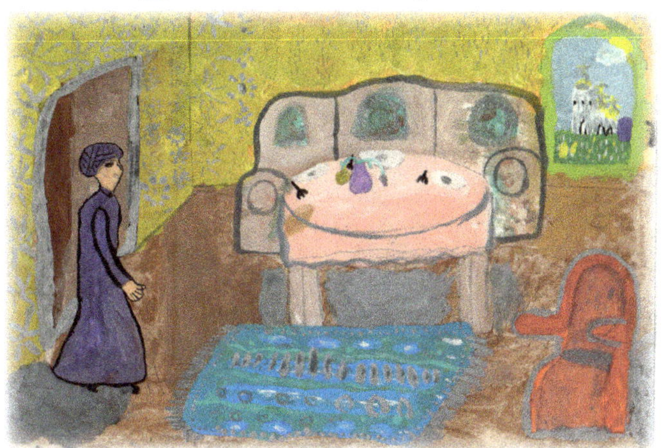

Julia Muraviova, age 9, 16 x 11.25 in. tempera

But he grabbed the rope to the bier and pulled the ice sheet to shore, where villagers hauled him out and made the bier safe.

The soldier was blood streaked, and his clothes began to freeze. Women took him to a nearby hut to get warm, in the care of an old woman, and returned to the procession.

Unable to cross the river, the villagers left the bier and Ismail's body in their tumbledown mosque. They went to thank the soldier, but he was gone.

The old woman said, "His hair is like flax, his eyes blue as God's heaven." When he removed his undershirt to dry it, she noticed a cross around his neck. The old woman never asked his full name or just where he was going. He got warm and dry, and left. The Muslims looked everywhere for him, but could not find him.

Here's the other story. The old mosque had needed replacement for years, but there was not enough money. Finally, villagers collected enough money for materials and invited everyone to help with the work. All kinds of people responded: Muscovites, Ukrainians, Belorussians, and people of the Caucasus, friendly and not bothered about nationalities.

Vasis, who had donated a lot of money for the mosque, was asked to name it. He named it after his mother, and made it a gift to the village's mothers.

To many it also commemorates the help people of many nations gave one another, and honors people's faith in each other. For still others, it is a monument to Ismail the blacksmith and the heroism of a Christian Russian soldier.

I looked around the room again. A beam of light set the mosque in the photograph glowing with all the colors of the rainbow.

In memory of my mother, Khafiza Abdulonova, the blacksmith's granddaughter.

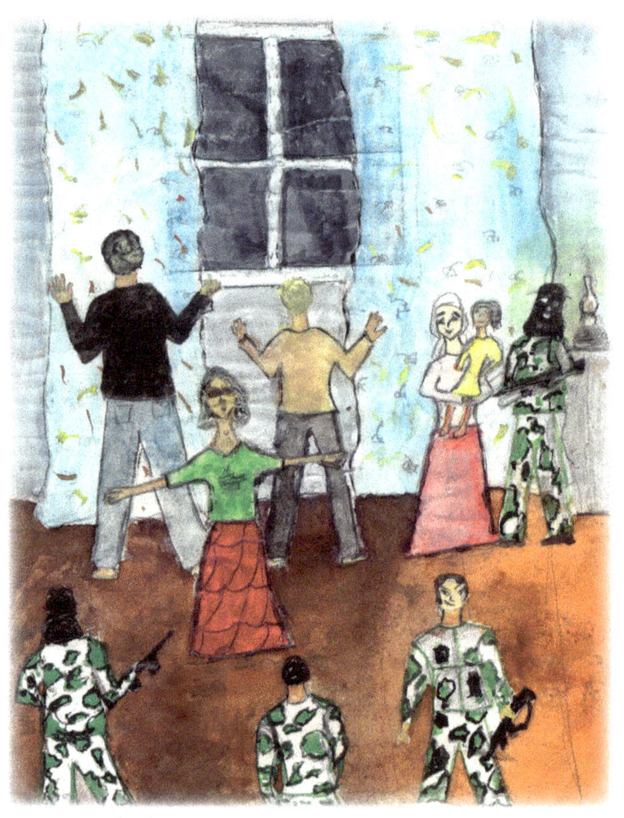

Ravzan Elnykoeya, age 13, 8 x 11.25 in. pencil & watercolor

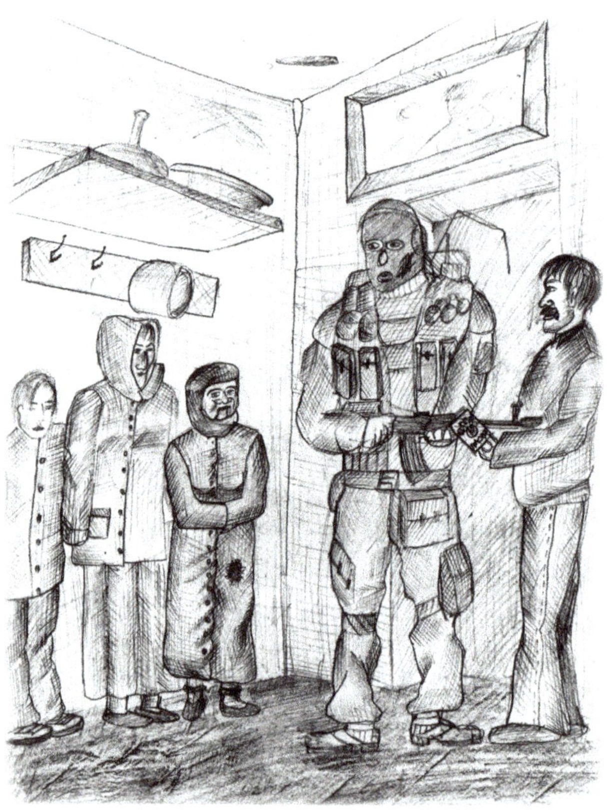

Artur Umarov, age14, 8.25 x 11.75 in. pencil

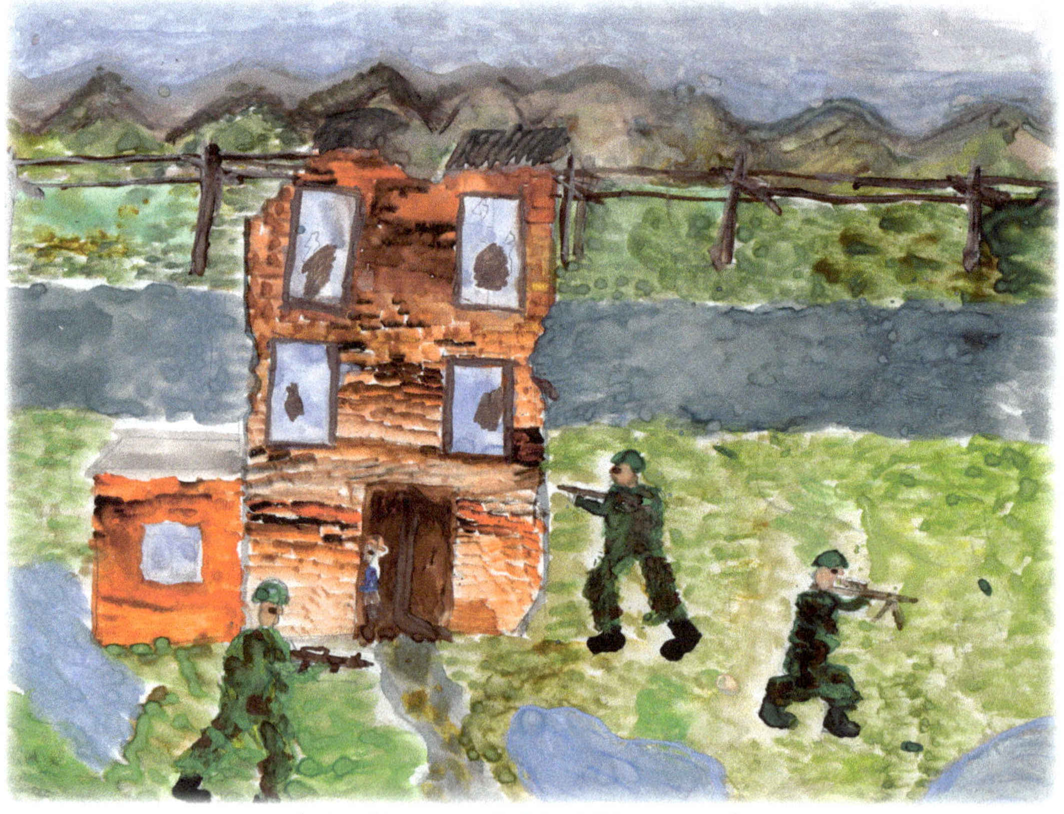

Artiom Ussov, age 9, 16 x 13 in. watercolor

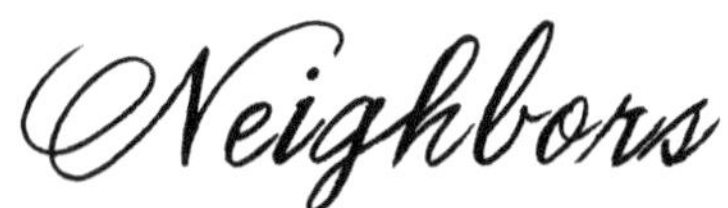

Neighbors

by Said Khamzat Nunuev, Chechnya

Saipudin had never liked Svetlana Viktorovna, the Russian schoolmistress.

"She doesn't like us Chechens," Saipudin said many times. "In 10 years she's never once asked us for salt or matches or a hammer. Why ever not? She seems like a stranger."

Even after hundreds of tanks appeared on the streets of Grozny, no one could have foreseen that this multinational city would be turned to dust. Saipudin did not want to take any risks. The five-story block where they lived was well away from the district where battle was raging; it had not suffered much. Saipudin took refuge in the cellar, with his wife Malika, his 16-year-old son Ali and his three-year-old daughter Prinesla, and other neighbors. Then one evening somebody reported that the Russian Special Forces were out hunting for Chechens and Ingush, people from the neighboring Republic of Ingushetia. "I don't believe it," Saipudin said, very worked up. But people insisted the 'mopping-up' had already begun on their street. Everyone must go upstairs to their apartments and meet the Special Forces with open doors; otherwise they would smash and burn everything.

Saipudin realized that he might never see his wife and children again. Then suddenly his neighbor Svetlana Viktorovna appeared. "Saipudin, I am afraid to be alone. Please come upstairs and stay with me, all of you. Malika! Ali! Let's go. Bring your sister with you." The Special Forces broke into the stairwell at midnight, and tramped upstairs.

"Your papers! Any Chechens or Ingush?" shouted a red-haired commando.

Svetlana Viktorovna came forward, "All our papers are in order. This is my husband, Sasha. And these are his sister and her children."

"Show me your papers!" The soldier shouted at Saipudin and his son.

"Here's my passbook." Saipudin handed over his passbook.

"A Chechen," the soldier said. "You come with me. Is the boy a Chechen too?"

Svetlana erupted, "I'll never let you take my husband away, or the boy either. These are my people. Sit down and have a rest. By the grace of God, I'll make you as welcome as I can."

She continued, "I'm ready to die with these people. If you want to shoot, shoot me first, a schoolteacher who's spent 28 years teaching children to be good and behave sensibly."

"All right. You can stay alive," said the commando, lowering his gun. "Let's go, guys."

Two years went by, and Grozny was back in the hands of Chechens. One night, Saipudin woke his wife up. "Listen! There's shouting in Svetlana's flat. Let's go see what's happening." The noise got louder, the cries more desperate. Saipudin rushed through his neighbor's open door. Two masked men had thrown Svetlana Viktorovna down and were tying her up. A third one with a gun was standing at the door. Saipudin realized that these were typical young thugs.

"Let her go at once. Aren't you ashamed? Don't you fear God?" Saipudin yelled.

The man at the door took aim at Saudipin's head. If Ali and Malika had not rushed into the room, he would have opened fire. The three of them dragged the attackers off Svetlana. Other neighbors appeared. The three masked men ran for the door, but as they made their escape one of them suddenly fired a single shot at Saipudin.

Within a month, Saipudin was home from the hospital. He, his family, and Svetlana decided to spend summer vacation together, in the mountains with his family, or by the Volga River with her aunt. There's lots of room everywhere, when we open our hearts.

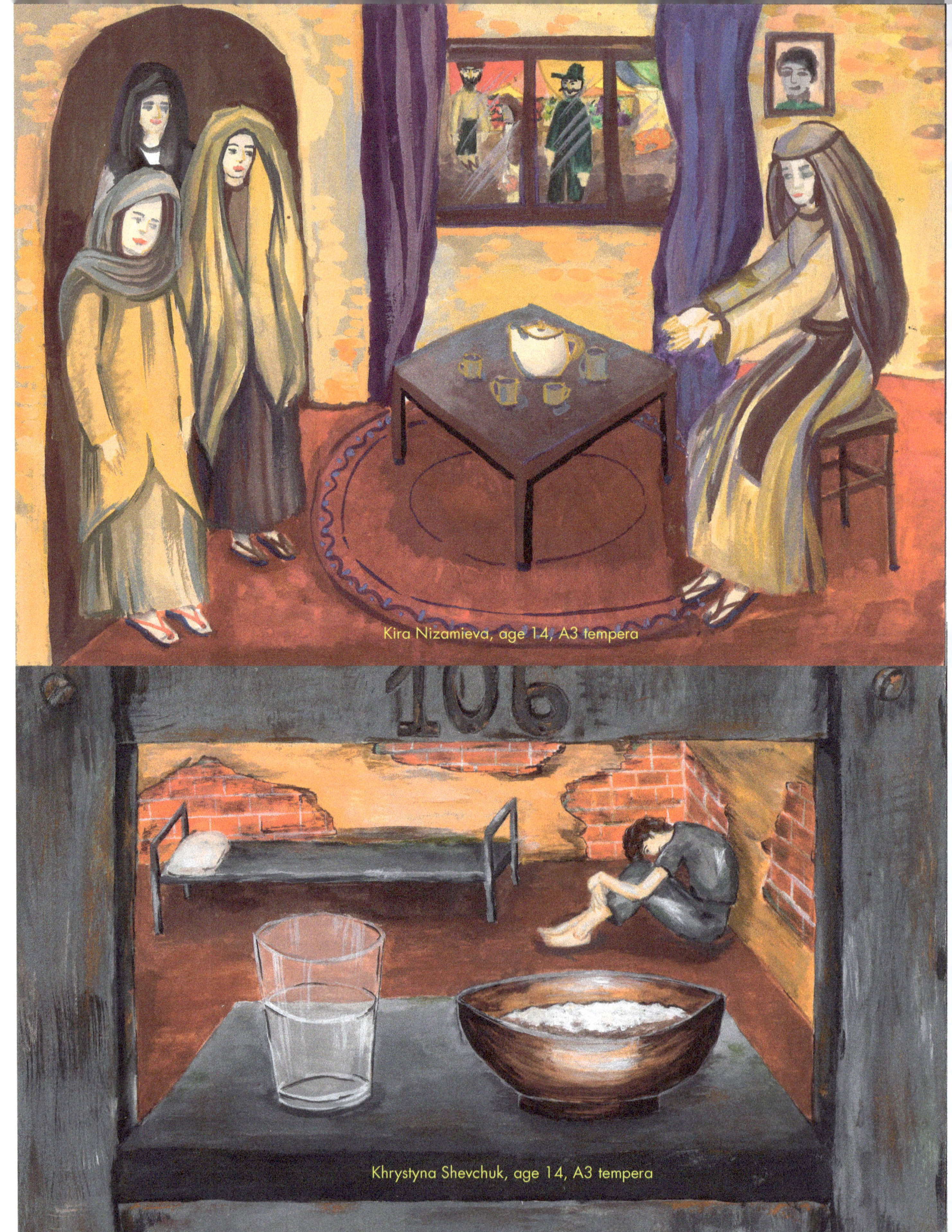

Kira Nizamieva, age 14, A3 tempera

Khrystyna Shevchuk, age 14, A3 tempera

The Price of Peace

a story of Ali Abu Awwad, Palestine, as told by Nadine Hoover

The phone rang in our Palestinian home. My mother answered. A group of Israeli Bereaved Families were calling to ask if they could visit. A year earlier, my beloved older brother Yusef was killed. While driving home, he came between children throwing stones and the Israeli army blocking entry into our town in the West Bank. He was shot by an Israeli soldier. Now, these Israeli women and men wanted to visit. They wanted to talk about our lost children, not only their own.

When Israel was created, Palestine lost its identity. We became refugees on our own land. We lost our identity, freedom to travel, and the right to enjoy the fruits of our labor. So of course we resisted. My courageous mother became a resistance leader and our home an office for the Palestinian Liberation Organization.

When the military takes over, they control every move, and rob you of your rights and humanity. Childhood is forbidden. When I turned 15 years old, I found a way to channel the anger that had taken over my life. I joined the Palestinian Uprising of 1987!

My mother and I were arrested and sentenced to ten years in 1990. Palestinian political prisoners created a moral, educated environment, full of Palestine's most-educated people–professors, doctors, and intellectuals, who raised the rest of us. For three years my mother and I asked to see one another, but the Israelis refused. So my mother and I started a hunger strike. After 17 days, the Israelis allowed us to visit.

I was shocked. The only time I'd ever gotten anything from an Israeli was from a nonviolent action! I assumed that violence was the only answer to violence. I asked myself, "Do I want to be right, or do I want to succeed?"

They released my mother and me two years later. I was 22 years old. Although I dream of organizing a nonviolent resistance movement, within six years after our release from prison the second Intifada of 2000 threw us into madness. It would be many years before we could organize the Taghyeer (Change) Movement.

I was shot in the knee and taken to a hospital in Saudi Arabia. I was recovering there when my older brother was killed at the blockade to our town.

I wanted revenge. What punishment would heal this wound? How many hearts needed to be broken to heal my heart? Then I realized, there is no number. The death of every Israeli would not be enough to bring back my brother. I felt trapped.

A year later, I was 29 years old when the phone rang. I thought, of course my mother would refuse this group of Israeli Bereaved Families in outrage. But she agreed.

"How could you agree to let them visit, mother?" I asked.

She looked surprised, "We're good Muslims. We honor visitors and offer them tea."

I couldn't believe it! I wasn't sure I could stand it. During their visit, I began to shake when I saw them cry. I had never imagined Jewish people had tears until that moment. That's when I realized what was different about this visit: their respect. They had not come in smashing things and arresting people. They called ahead to ask if they could visit. They spoke respectfully. I felt another deep, inner change.

I realized that the only cure for people robbed of humanity, was to restore our humanity. I wanted to connect with the community–all the communities, people like me and not like me, who agree with me and disagree with me. The checkpoints were machines of hatred, so I wanted to see peace workers near the checkpoints where there are Israeli soldiers. This was the place to act, all of us together.

We dedicated Abu Awwad family land, near the Gush Etzion junction, as the Karama (Dignity) Nonviolence Center. There, we agreed to share stories truthfully and listen respectfully, believing the story was true for the speaker, as long as each speaker also listened respectfully and believed others' stories were true for them. It's painful. It's not easy.

But we have found the beginnings of peace in this place, where we stop and listen to one another. Peace is possible when two truths finally fit together in one place. But for this to happen, Palestinians must voice the Palestinian truth, resist occupation, and peacefully lead the way to our freedom. Whatever the price of peace, it's better than the price of war.

Part 2: Healing Ourselves and the Earth

Stories from Chechnya, Kenya, Ukraine, and USA

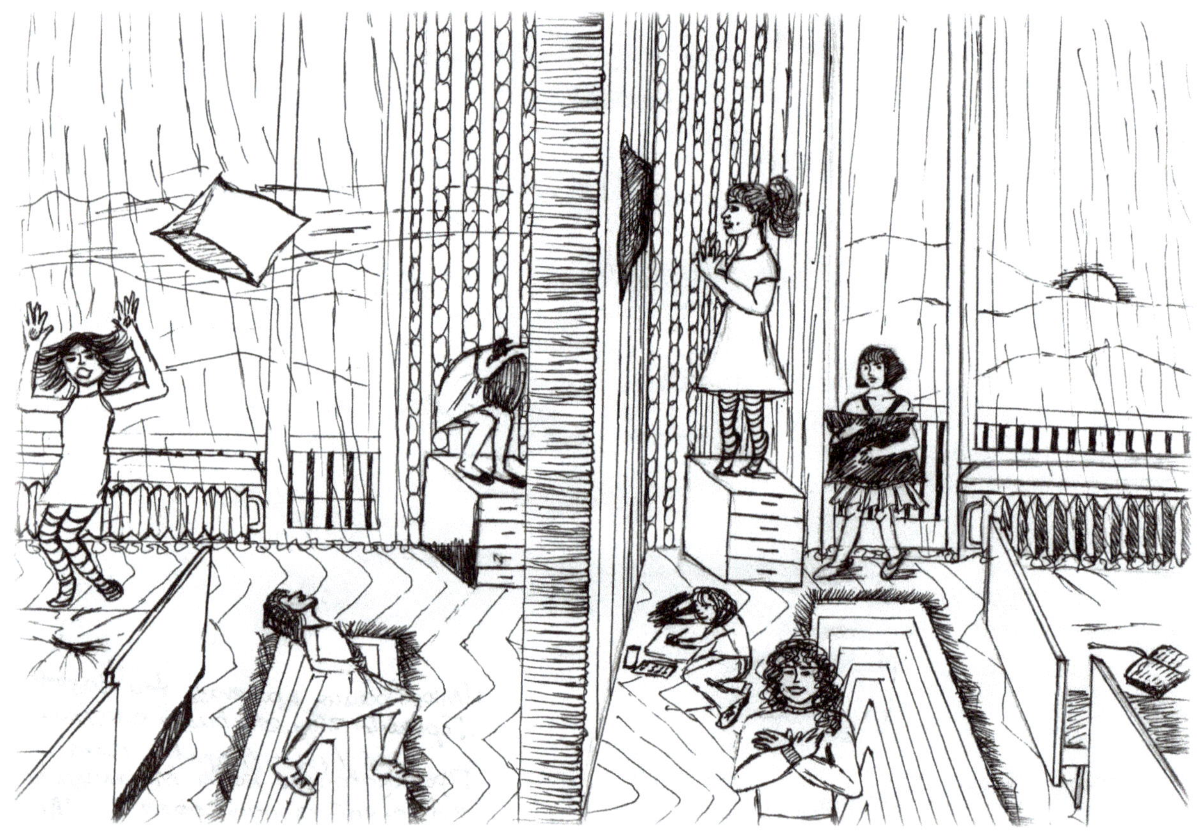

Asya Umarova, age 16, 11.5 x 8.25 in. ink

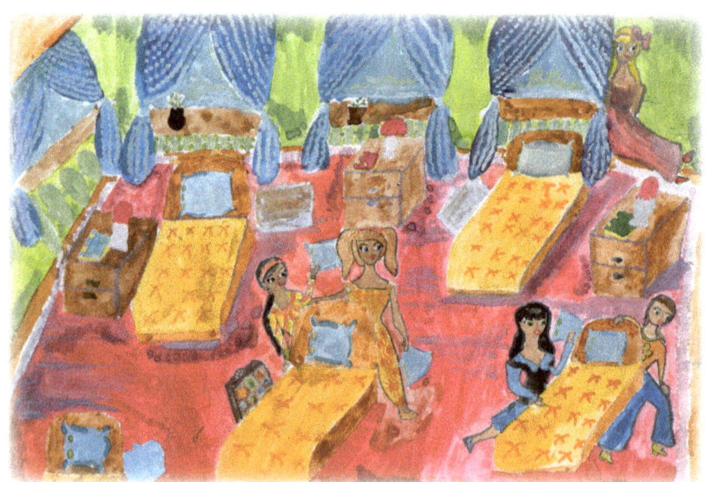

Kira Lalina, age 9, 16.5 x 11.5 in. tempera

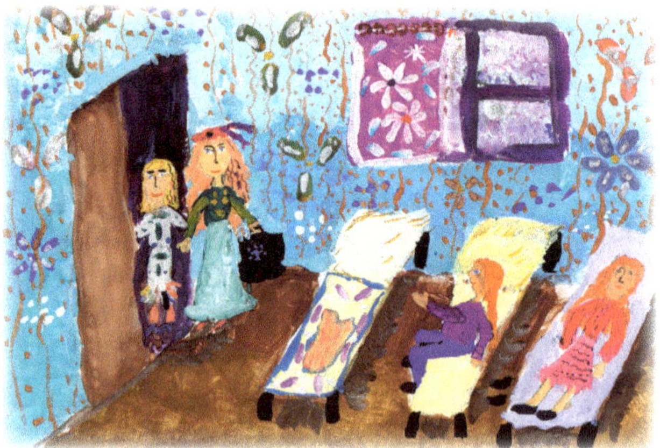

Ania Katsman, age 9, 16.5 x 11.5 in. tempera

First Bitter, Then Sweet

by Asya Vasaeva, Chechnya

The Chechen children were cold mostly, and always hungry. Many homes were damaged. Families who were used to four rooms were crowded into one. Then a miracle: Seda, Luisa, and a dozen other girls were chosen to attend a holiday camp called Blue Wave.

It was beautiful and safe. There was plenty of food. Although their dormitory was scruffy, damp, and chilly, it was big. Each girl had a bed, and room for her things. A big hole in the wall needed a pillow in it to keep out the draft and the noise from the next room, but it was almost heaven compared with home.

Then it changed. Luisa and Seda were in the dormitory when several Russian girls burst in. "Which of you came sneaking into our room?" one screamed. They claimed that their dormitory had been turned upside down and that things were missing, and would not listen to Seda and Luisa's denials.

"That's a lie," they said. "One of us spotted one of you coming out of our room. We know you have been stealing!"

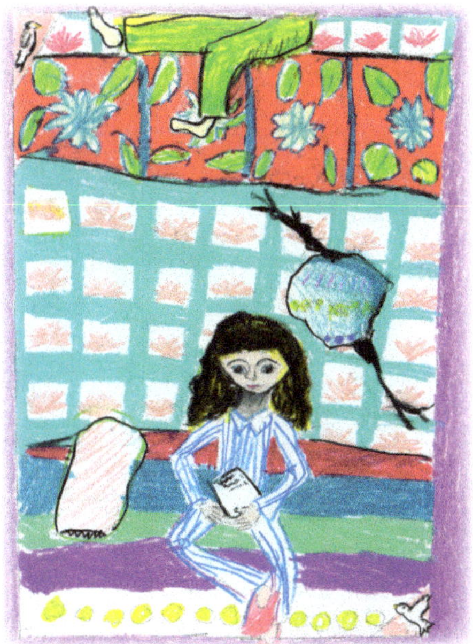

Alhazur Karemov, age 9, 8.5 x 11 in. colored pencil and pastel

House Five was divided between Chechens and Russians. Neither side missed a chance to "get at" the other, everywhere – bathroom, dining hall, game room. It spilled into the dormitory. All night the pillow was flung from one side to the other, so cold drafts and colder feelings came through.

The Chechens complained to the teachers, who made a search. Only the Chechens' things were found in their quarters. The teachers spoke to the Russians, "How could you think of making others in the same house look bad? They are innocent, and have already suffered much. War destroyed their houses. They could not go to school. Some of their parents have been killed; some have lost both. Yet you insulted them cruelly. You must have hearts of stone to do this."

Insults and name-calling stopped. The girls started talking to each other, then playing games and walking together. One day Seda said to Vika, one of the accusers, "Why did you start all that?"

Vika explained, "An older boy told us all Chechens are beggars who take anything they can and make trouble if they get a chance. We had to get you out. Now we know that was wrong. We want to make up for what we did."

They invited Seda, Luisa, and the others to move into their dormitory, which was warmer and more comfortable, and did their best to help the Chechens feel at home. Soon they were fascinated by stories about the war and life in that ravaged land.

Then Vika had to leave, with no time to say goodbye. The girls missed her. No one could be bored when she was around. Seda found a farewell note under her pillow, "Seda, I love you very, very, very much. Don't forget your friends. Write."

The rest of the time passed quickly. Even the house parents cried when it was time to leave. No one would forget their experiences or new friends.

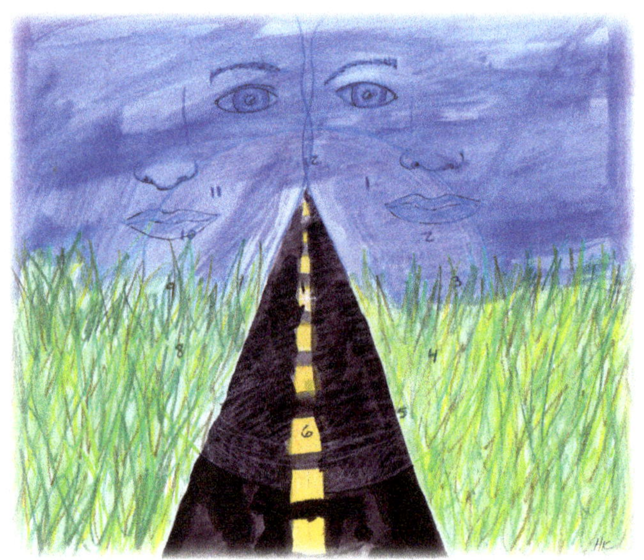

Heather Kroger, age 17, 13.5 x 11.5 in
watercolor and colored pencil

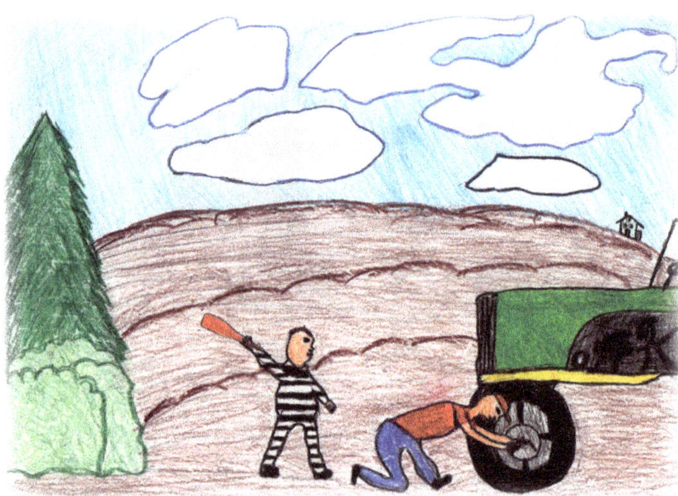

Matthew Ward, age 11, 11 x 8.5 in. colored pencil

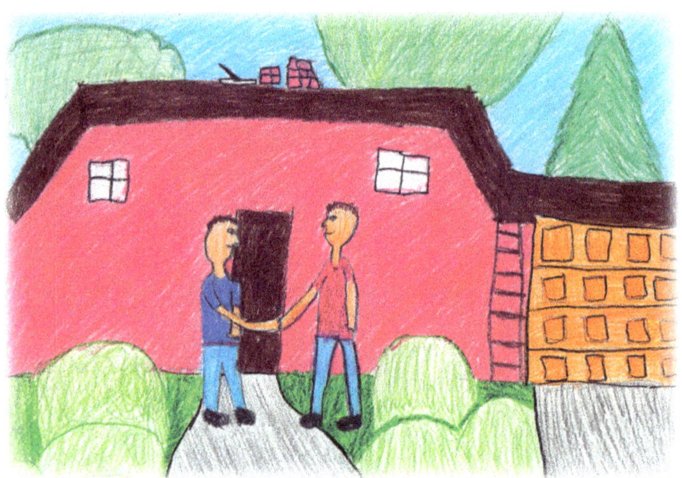

Matthew Ward, age 11, 11 x 8.5 in. colored pencil

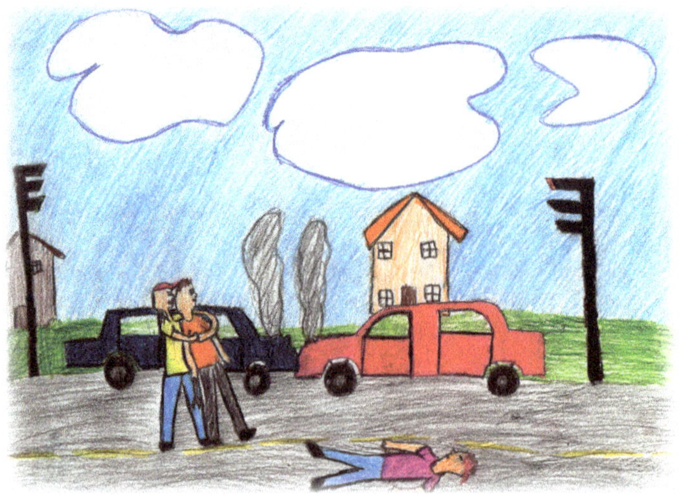

Matthew Ward, age 11, 11 x 8.5 in. colored pencil

He was Ready to Hit Me

by Calhoun Geiger, United States of America

One day in spring 1947 I was in Florida, plowing a field for a friend. I had been a conscientious objector during World War II, and was happy to be home, farming, again.

A group of convicts was working near the field. I stopped near some bushes hedging that side of the field to adjust the plow. A man came from the bushes, wearing a convict's uniform, carrying a tool handle as a heavy club. He stopped near me and said, "I need money bad, and whatever you have, I'm going to take."

I said, "If you need help that badly, just say so, and we won't have any rough stuff." I went back to work.

He lowered his club.

I said, "You're running away. Do you realize you will be hunted?" He said yes, but the chain gang bosses were mean. We talked while I worked. Suddenly he dropped the club. "You win," he said. "I'm going back." He disappeared into the bushes. After a prayer of thanks, I kept plowing.

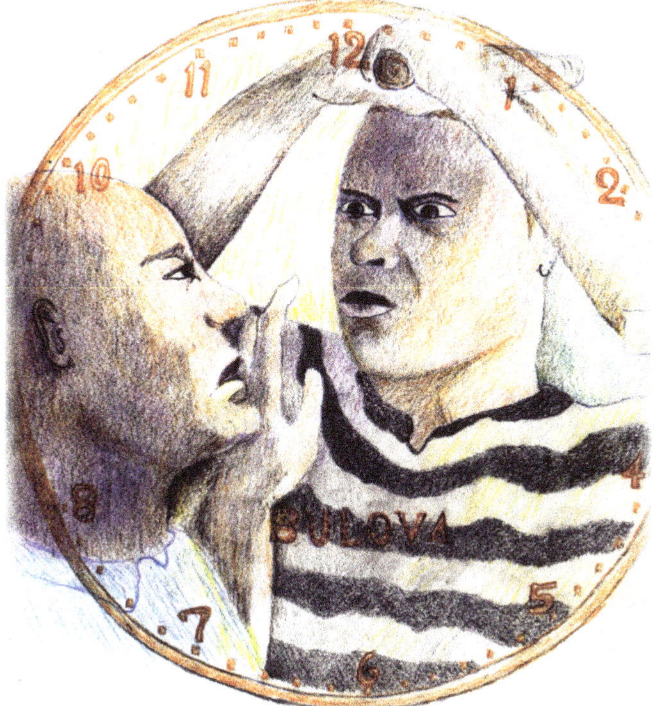

Marco Chacon, age 16, lost original, colored pencil

Several years later, I was on my way home, nearing an intersection, when two cars crashed there. The drivers ran at each other, fists flying. One went down. The other kicked him and struck him with a wrench.

I was tempted to go home, but an inner voice urged, "No! Stop and help!" There was no time to find a phone to call the police. The inner voice spoke again: "You are strong. Move quickly!"

From behind I wrapped my arms around the attacker. He struggled, but I held on, not hurting him. When someone nearby offered help. I asked him to call the police. When I explained what had happened, they let me go home. Later, I regretted that I had not looked at either man's face.

Several years later a worker called from a local mental hospital where I volunteered to say George Harris, a former patient, had recognized me there. I said I didn't know any George Harris. The hospital worker said Harris told her he was the escaped prisoner, and the driver who would have killed the other if I had not intervened.

Harris said when he got out of hospital, he went to work and started saving money. Now he wanted to mail a gift for me – a very nice watch.

He wrote periodically to say he was doing well, and sent beautiful gifts several times. I always responded with thanks to the return address. He never replied, but one day a car pulled up and the driver said, "Cal Geiger …I believe."

"Yes," I said, "and who are you?"

"George Harris," he answered.

He had become a teacher, and had a wife and children. His health was poor now. He wanted to see and thank me before dying. He walked to his car and left. What one says and does can make a big difference. I made a difference for George Harris, but also for myself. I am overwhelmingly grateful I knew him.

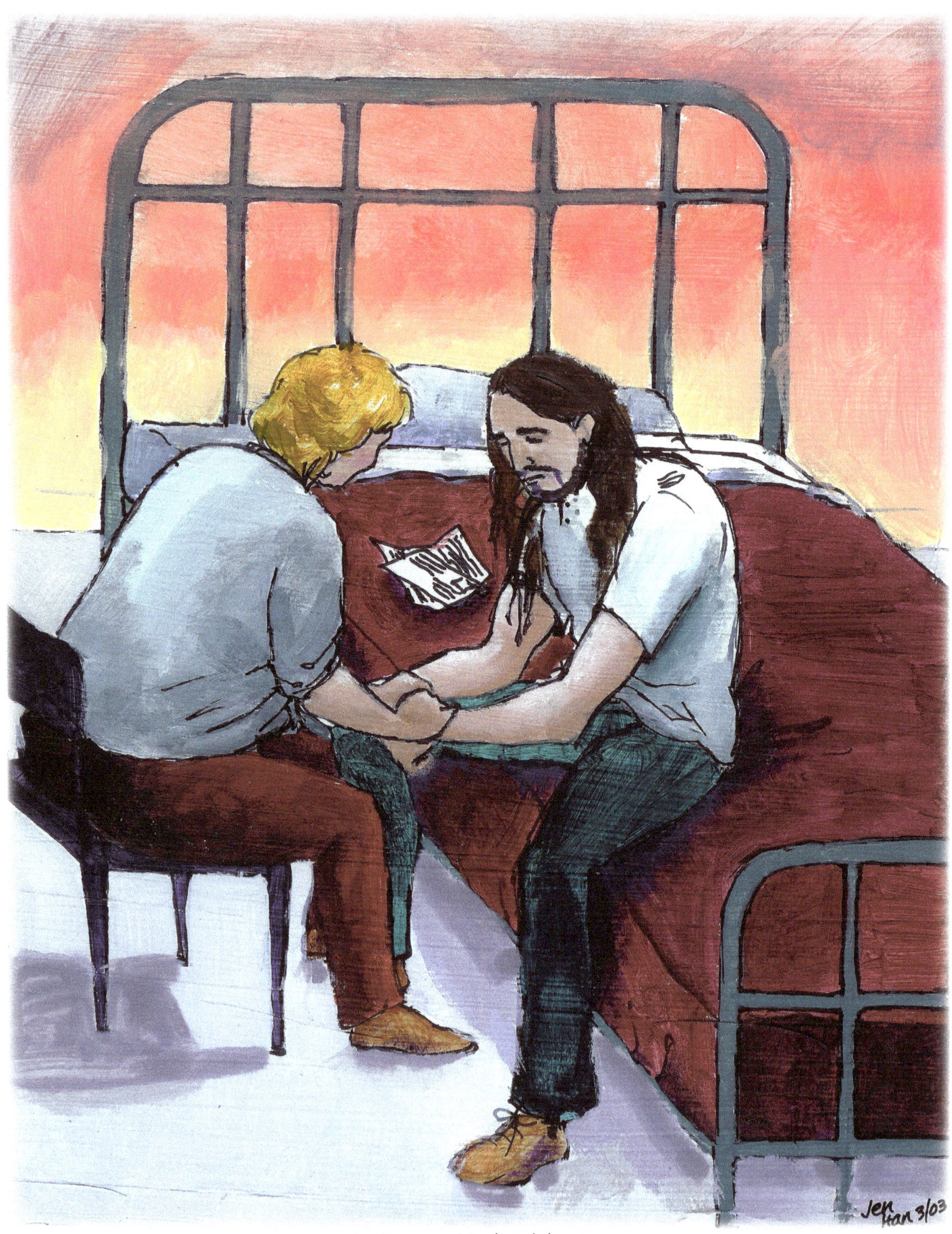

Jen Han, age 17, digital drawing

The Healing Power of Forgiveness

by Aba Gayle, United States of America

Detective Landry was gentle as he spoke those terrible words: "I'm sorry, but your daughter, Catherine, is dead. She was murdered, stabbed to death."

My heart broke. My brain couldn't think. Nothing was real. Surely I would wake to find the nightmare was over. I couldn't let anyone hug me for fear I would break. I couldn't cry for fear someone might hear. With the shower running full blast, I screamed and screamed and screamed. People thought I was fine, but a deep, dark rage boiled. All I thought about was revenge for the death of my beloved child.

Douglas Mickey was arrested, tried, convicted, and sentenced to death. People said once this villain was executed, I would be well again. Not knowing any better, I believed them. So, I waited, and I hated.

After eight long years of darkness, I took my first step toward healing. In a meditation course I sat, quieted my head, and was present. I began taking mother to church. I found not only myself, but the image of God in me. I became aware of being a beloved child of God.

I saw an interview with a Jewish holocaust survivor. He forgave not only the German people, but the actual guards who killed his whole family. When I heard his testimony of forgiveness, something in me became clear. I thought perhaps I could forgive the man who murdered Catherine.

One evening a friend suggested that I let the murderer know of my intent. I was outraged! No way would I communicate with him. This was between God and me.

But as I drove home, I heard a voice, "You must forgive him, and let him know!" The voice was so loud and convincing I didn't sleep. At four in the morning, I found myself typing a letter to the man who murdered Catherine.

I can still feel the shivers going down my spine as I closed the mailbox. All the anger, rage, and lust for revenge simply vanished. In its place was the most wonderful feeling of joy and peace. I knew, in that holy instant, no one had to be executed for me to heal. I had been healed by the simple act of offering forgiveness.

To my surprise, I received a gentle and kind rely. Douglas expressed sorrow for his crime, adding that he understood how empty such words might sound. He wrote, "Gayle, your letter meant more to me than I can ever tell you. The knowledge that I inflicted such terrible pain on you was a burden my heart and soul could not bear. Your letter of forgiveness released me of that pain. Knowing you were able to deal with Catherine's death and find new sources of love and wisdom gave me exquisite pleasure and released my soul's agony. I would gladly give my life, this instant, if it would in any way change that terrible night." I realized that the night Catherine lost her life, Douglas lost his future.

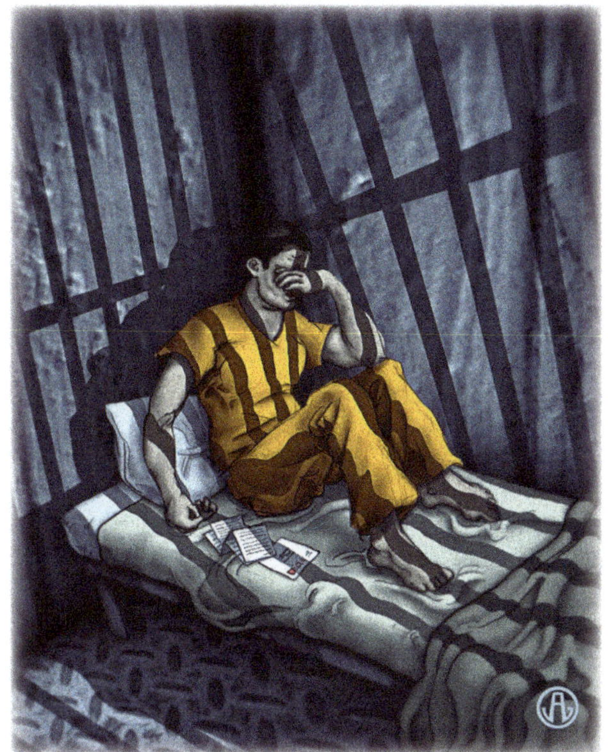

Joe Golling, age 18, digital drawing

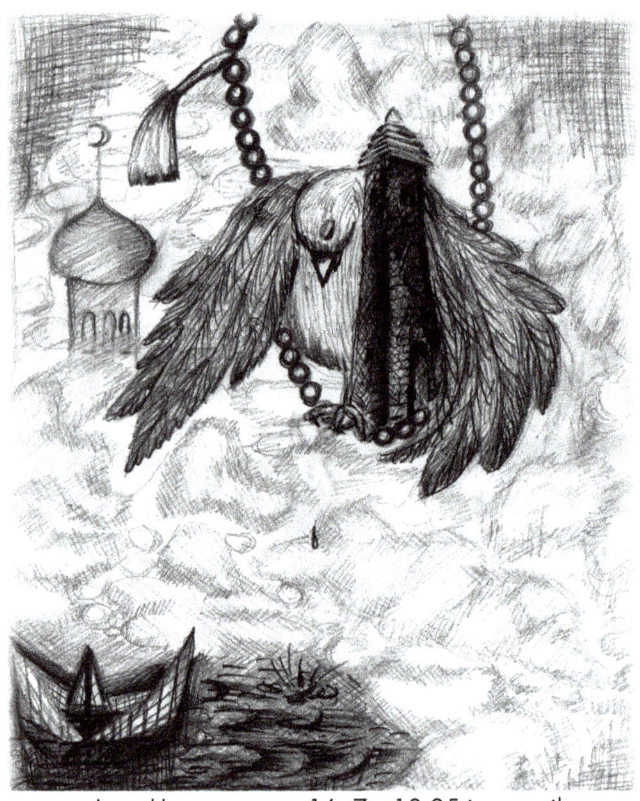

Asya Umarova, age 16, 7 x 10.25 in. pencil

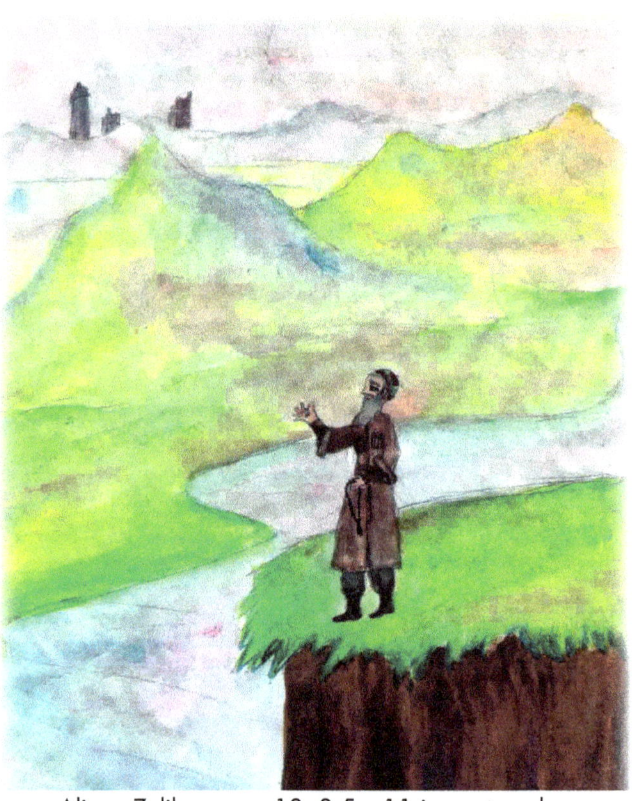

Alieva Zulihan, age 18, 8.5 x 11 in. watercolor

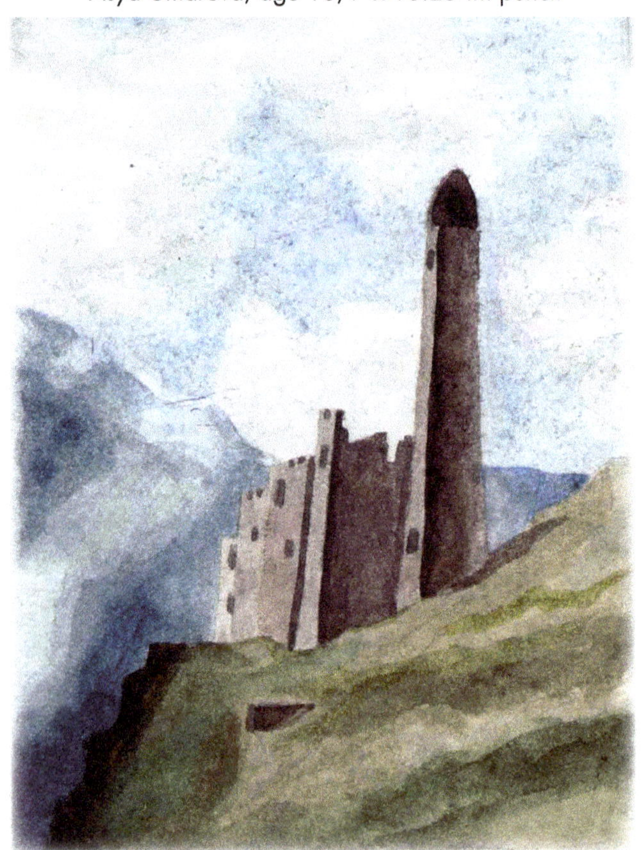

Oznieva Aset, age 17, watercolor

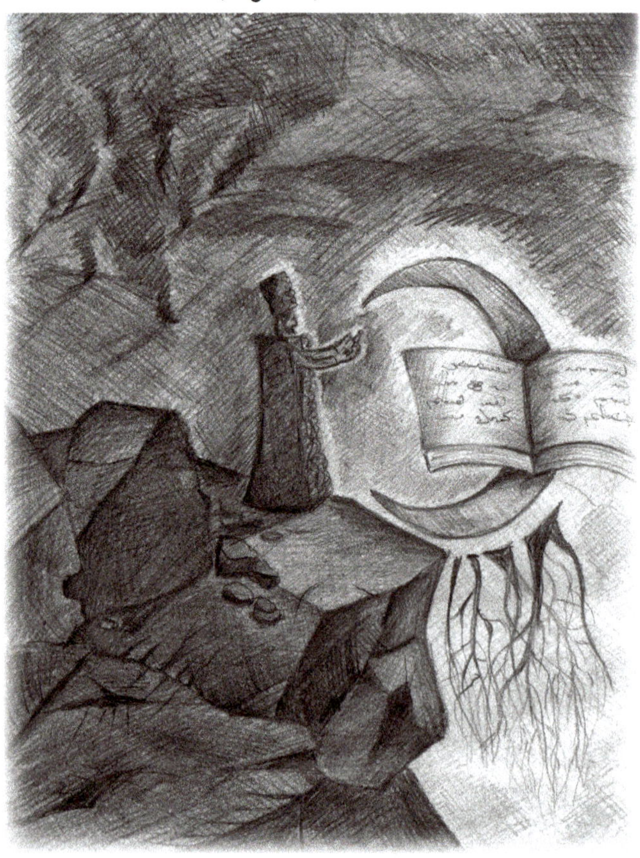

AsyaYmarova, age 16, 7.5 x 11.5 in. pencil

Kunta-hadji

by Said Khamzat Nunuev, Chechnya

"Tie a turban round your heart, before you tie it on your head."
"Do you desire to love Allah the Almighty?
Then you must love righteousness."

The most distinguished Chechen saint, Sheikh Kunta-hadji, was born about 1830 in the village of Isti Su. A Sufi and founder of the Student Brotherhood, he is recognized and revered throughout the Islamic world.

As a child, Kunta-hadji migrated with his parents to the village of Isklan Urt, in the mountains at the heart of Chechen territory. While a young man, he began preaching and teaching.

In those days Chechens were worn down, driven to desperation, by war with Russia. Then they heard Kunta-hadji's message of peace, tranquillity, concord, and unity, through faith and goodwill. Kunta-hadji's teachings saved the Chechens' soul from unimaginable miseries, in his day and in the days to follow.

Even as a child, Kunta-hadji questioned his elders: Why do people make war? Why kill each other? Why is there evil? Why doesn't God wipe out all vices? As he grew up, Kunta-hadji sought answers to his questions in the religious books of the Zhains and in Arabia from enlightened Sheikhs taught in Islam's best schools. He returned to Chechnya in the mid-1800s as a Sufi, a peace-loving form of Islam.

The War of the Caucasus raged in Chechnya and Dagestan. The Imam Shamil led the mountain peoples to resist Russia by armed force. But Kunta-hadji sought a peaceful resolution. He knew all-out resistance could lead to Chechens' annihilation. He sought to turn the highlanders towards peace.

The outcome of the controversy between Shamil and Kunta-hadji is clear. The Russians' overwhelming strength and cruelty broke the mountain people's long resistance. Shamil became an honoured guest of the Russian Tsar and ended his days in the holy city of Mecca. Kunta-hadji, a lifelong preacher of reconciliation, peace, generosity, and justice, was arrested by order of Tsar Alexander II in winter 1864. He was imprisoned, and suffered the fate of a common criminal: loneliness, cold, and hunger. A few of his letters reached his family bearing witness to his trials, which he underwent with dignity and patience.

People of many faiths have called for humans to strive for goodness, compassion, and generosity, including the Russian Christian Leo Tolstoy, the Indian Hindu Mahatma Gandhi, and the Chechen Sufi Kunta-hadji.

To this day Chechens remember his words:

Overcome evil with kindness and love.
Overcome greed through generosity.
Overcome falsehood by truth-telling.
Overcome unbelief through faith.
~ Kunta-hadji

A kind word can move a mountain.
Everything passes away, but goodness is eternal.
Take time before you do harm; waste no time to do good.
A good neighbor is more use than a faraway brother.
A kind word is a priceless treasure.
~ Chechen Proverbs

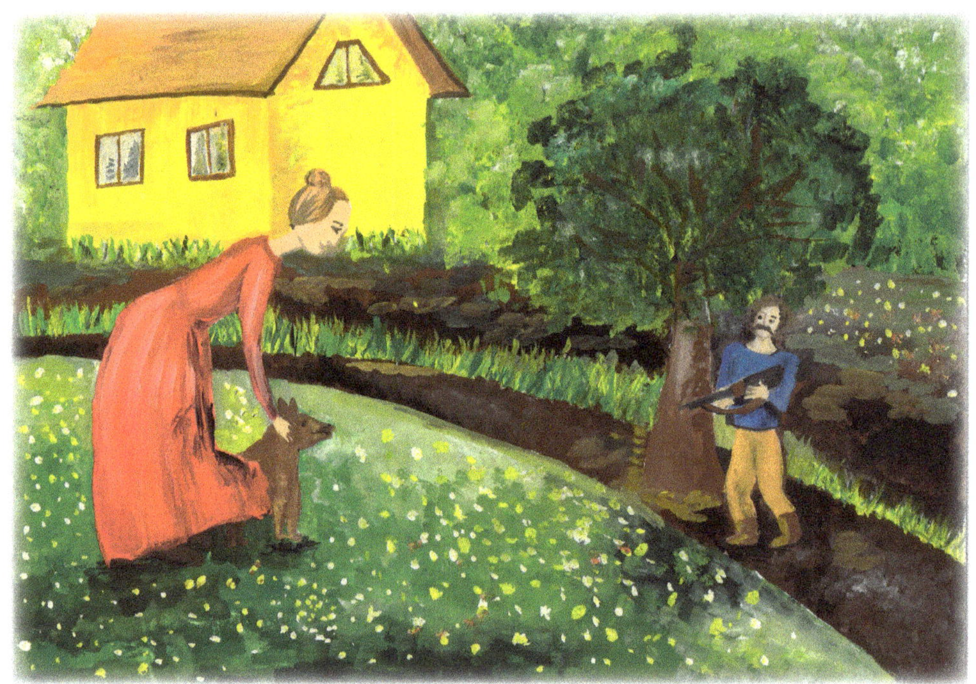

Sofija Gochachko, age 13, A3 tempera

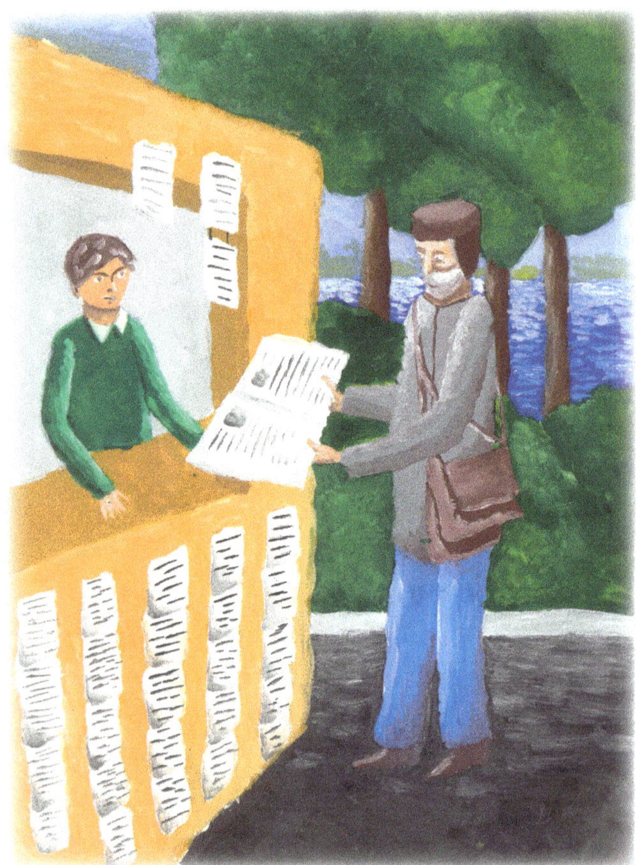

Danik Dovhun, age 14, A3 tempera

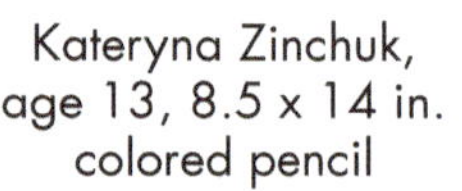

Kateryna Zinchuk,
age 13, 8.5 x 14 in.
colored pencil

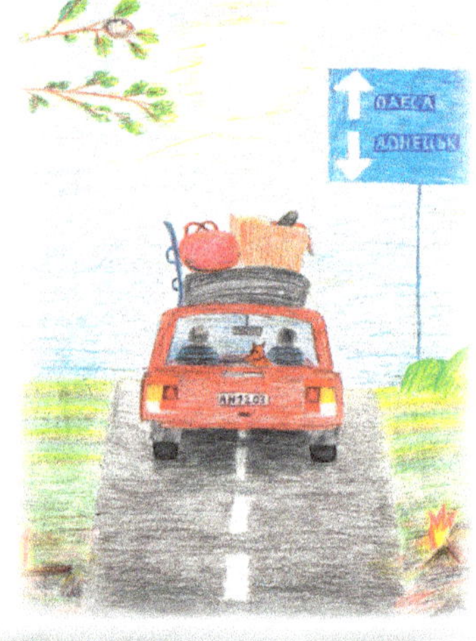

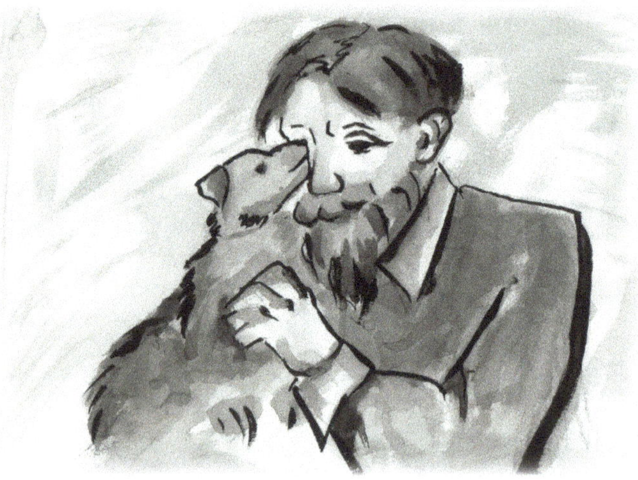

Anastasia Hrihorenko, age 17, A3 pen & ink

Love of Life

by Inna Ischuk, Ukraine

Vladimir Alekseevich closed the heavy door of the Institute of Entrepreneurship for the last time. As founder and rector of the Institute, he was sad. War had come to their hometown, Donetsk, as hostilities spread into eastern Ukraine. He and his wife had both lost their jobs.

On his way home, Vladimir heard the familiar whistle, and then an explosion. He threw himself onto the grass to wait for the attack to pass. Then, he saw black smoke rising from his apartment. Vladimir rushed to the entrance hall, but the firefighters stopped him.

"Where's my wife?" He shouted, "Nadya? Nadya?"

"I am here," Nadya said quietly. "Luckily, I went out to buy sour cream for the borsch tonight." Vladimir hugged his wife tight. The apartment was destroyed. At 70, Vladimir had no work or home. He felt cast off, shipwrecked. Nadya was all he had left. "Thank God, we're alive," she said gently. "Let's go to the summer cottage. We can live there." Vladimir took the car from the garage. They drove thirty kilometers out of Donetsk to the village.

Their son was studying at Odesa University. He had invited them to stay with him, but they couldn't imagine moving to a strange city with no friends, community, or work. The cottage was near the front line. The constant shelling often drove Vladimir and Nadya into the cellar, terrified. Vladimir's soul felt empty and lost.

"We'll die here," Nadya whispered.

"Life is over," said Vladimir helplessly.

One day, Nadya saw a stray dog weaving through the potato plants in the kitchen garden. When she heard shots in the yard, she ran out. Vladimir hurried after her, "Where are you going?"

She ran towards the big, red dog, who was miraculously dodging the bullets from a neighbor's rifle. His fur was full of burrs and his eyes glittered. The dog ran to hide under her skirt. "Is it yours?" the neighbour asked sternly.

"Yes," Nadya answered firmly, "He's ours!"

"Watch it. He was digging up my potatoes. Next time I'll shoot him." After the neighbor left, the dog came out from under her skirt, panting and wagging his tail.

"You're so smart!" Nadya smiled. "This is how one should love life!" Vladimir looked at his neighbour then at the dog, then burst into laughter, "We should love life like that!"

He looked at the bright sun in the sky and took a deep breath. The darkness in his soul began to melt. Vladimir proposed, "Let's go to our son in Odesa." Nadya smiled and tears glittered in her eyes.

They started out early the next morning with the dog as their mascot. They called him Druzhok, meaning friend. Odesa welcomed them with bright lights, jokes, and peace. Their son found an apartment for them to rent. Vladimir walked the streets freely, taking pictures of the old buildings. He loved the architecture and remembered how, as a child, he had dreamed of becoming a journalist. But technical university, community responsibilities, and family had taken priority.

While walking the dog, he would stop at a kiosk to buy the Porto-Franco newspaper. One day, he saw a free journalism course free for people internally displaced by the military operations. So he signed up.

He arrived at the Pravo Press Club an hour early. As the former Rector, becoming a student made him nervous. The other students were much younger.

The teacher described Odesa as a complicated and interesting city, with many opportunities. The first assignment was to write an essay about his life. Vladimir's spirits lifted. He took a pen and paper and the past poured onto the paper in lines and sentences forming a whole story.

The teacher asked each student to read their story. When Vladimir finished reading his, he felt relieved. The teacher smiled, "You have talent. You should go on writing." Inspired, Vladimir wrote each of his assignments with enthusiasm. He attended exhibitions and presentations, asked questions, and interviewed people. His life filled with new information and a new sense of drive and confidence.

He started a blog dedicated to city life and the interesting people of Odesa. He described the glorious architecture and colourful news from meet-the-artist sessions and presentations.

His wife found a new job teaching at a music school. In the evenings, the three, Vladimir, Nadya and Druzhok, walked around Odesa inspired by their love for life!

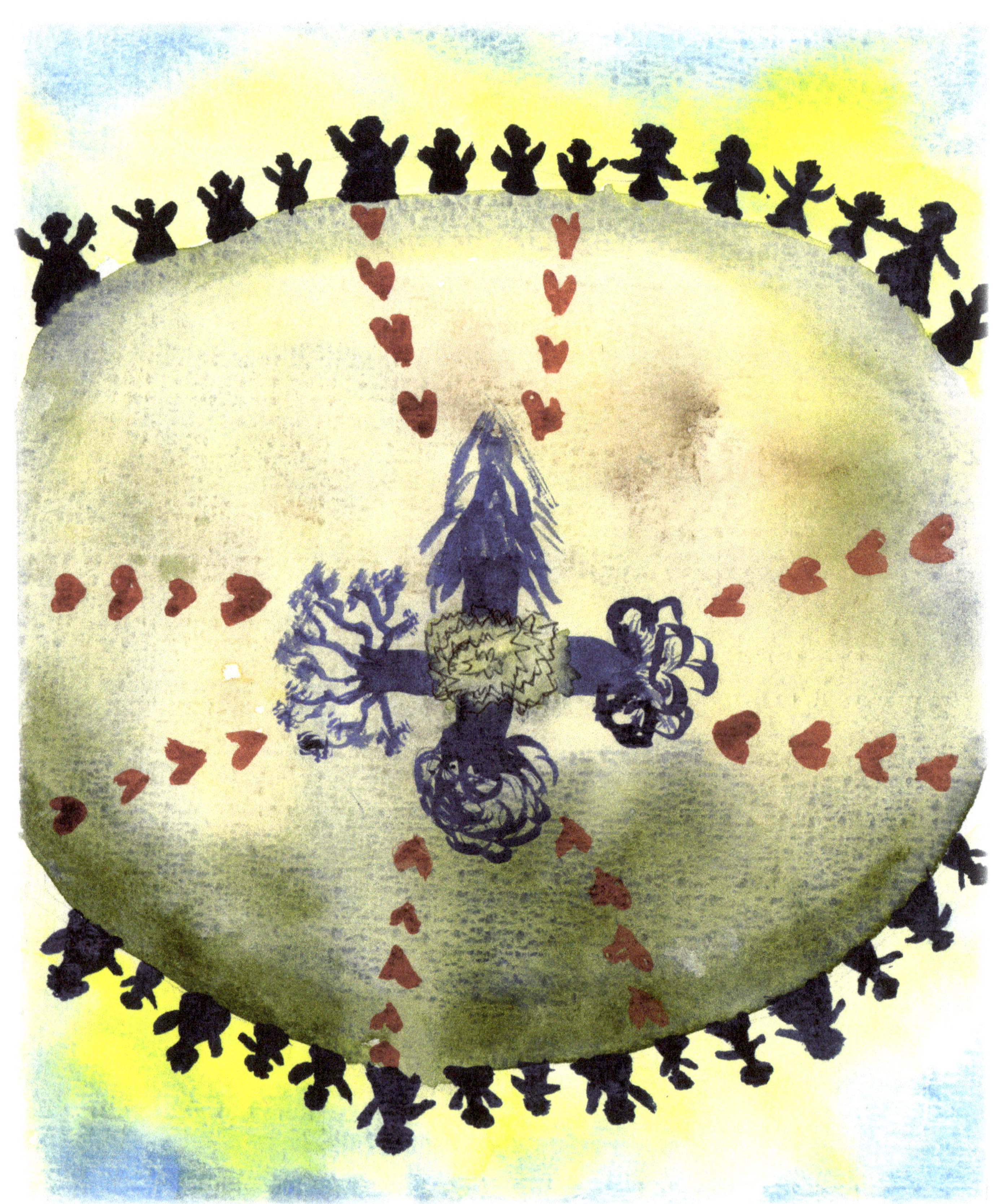

Maggie MacArthur-McKay, age 15, 6.5 x 8.75 in. watercolor

Planting Trees to Heal the Earth

by Janet Sabina and Marnie Clark, Kenya

In Kenya, as people crowd onto the land they cut trees for farmland and firewood. Without tree roots, heavy rains wash the soil away. Deserts appear where forests used to be.

Wangari Maathai wanted to improve the life of Kenya's people. She was told all the way through school that she would be a leader with the responsibility to help her people. This was not an easy job. She decided to help by planting LOTS of trees.

She got 6,000 free seedlings, but the people she found to plant them didn't have the tools or money to get the work done. And it was too dry to water them. All but two of the 6,000 seedlings died. This didn't work.

Wangari realized she couldn't do the work alone, so she started a committee of women. They got important leaders to plant trees in Kenya's capital to honor Kenyan heroes. But they didn't water the trees, and all of them died. This didn't work.

So then the committee set a goal of planting millions of trees on public land and having people living nearby care for them. The forestry department liked the plan and agreed to provide free seedlings. But in the end they couldn't afford it, so this didn't work either.

Wangari thought: Why not train women to start tree nurseries? Then they could earn money by supplying the trees. Finally, something worked!

Women learned to gather seeds from nearby trees, start seedlings, and take care of them. They learned to run their own small businesses. Their work was called the Green Belt Movement, and it was wonderful.

Soon people were planting native trees to make windbreaks, hold moisture in the soil, and produce firewood. All this was wonderful too. News of their successes spread, and meetings were held explaining the importance of trees. People across Kenya wrote asking for trees to plant and forming committees. The Green Belt people provided tools, water tanks, and training to people who took care of trees.

Some people planted seedlings with enthusiasm, but then got tired of caring for them and many seedlings died. So the Green Belt people offered to send money for each tree still alive six months after planting. This solution worked.

People brought in new kinds of trees that grew faster and could be cut and sold sooner than native Kenyan trees. But trees cut down so soon don't stop soil erosion. Also, Kenyan trees provide animal fodder, fruits, honey, and herbal medicines that the imported trees did not. The Green Belt people taught others about the benefits of native Kenyan trees.

Wangari's work has made a huge difference: over 1,500 tree nurseries began and over 10 million native trees were planted, mostly in Green Belts near schools. More than a million schoolchildren have helped care for trees.

Wangari received a $10,000 award for her work. People waited to hear how she would use it. She gave it to form new tree nurseries and Green Belt committees across Africa. Wangari cares for everyone and our precious Earth, and has experienced the extraordinary goodness and capabilities of ordinary people.

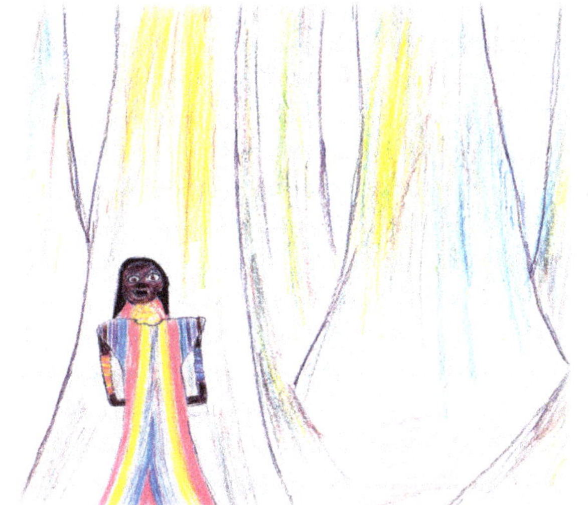

Aubrey Riley, age 11, 11 x 8.5 in. color pencil and marker

"There is no trust more sacred than

the one the world holds with children.

There is no duty more important than

ensuring that their rights are respected,

that their welfare is protected,

that their lives are free from fear and want

and that they grow up in peace."

~ Kofi A. Annan
Former Secretary General of the United Nations

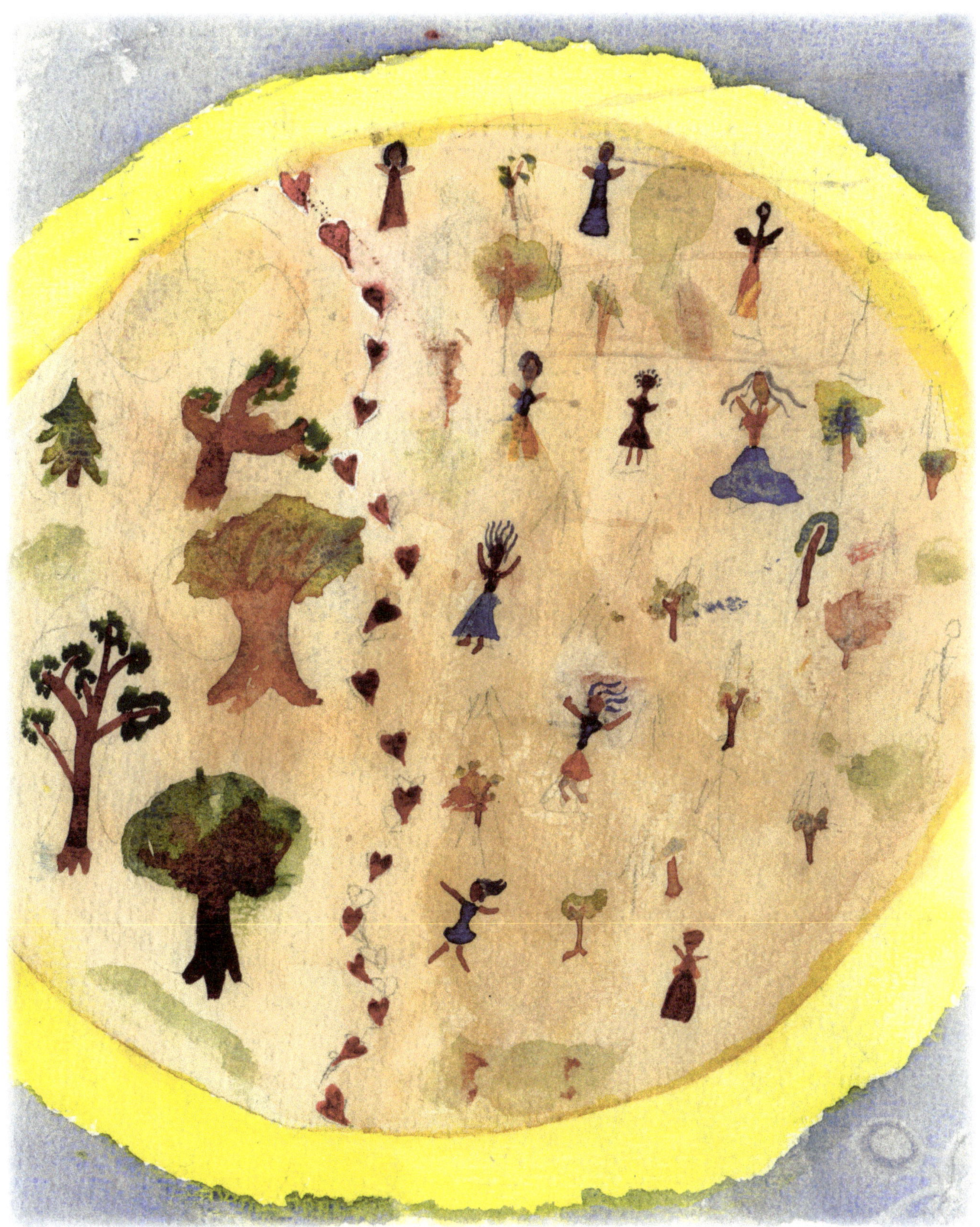

Maggie MacArthur-McKay, age 15, 6.5 x 8.75 in. watercolor

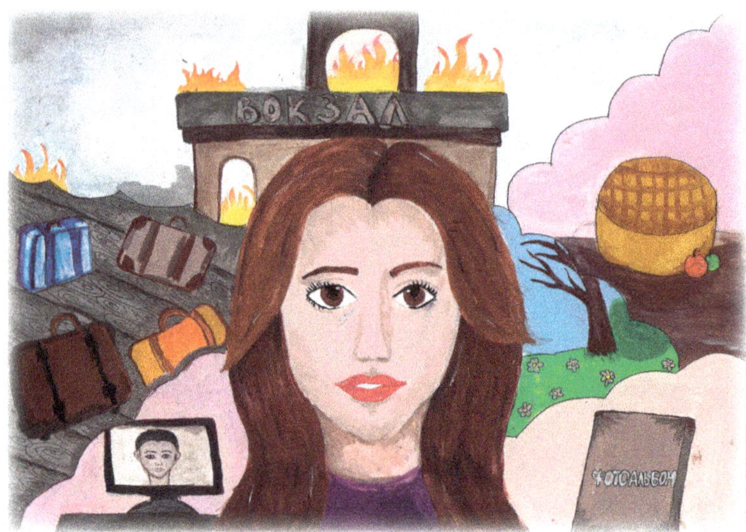

Drobot Daria, age15, tempera paint

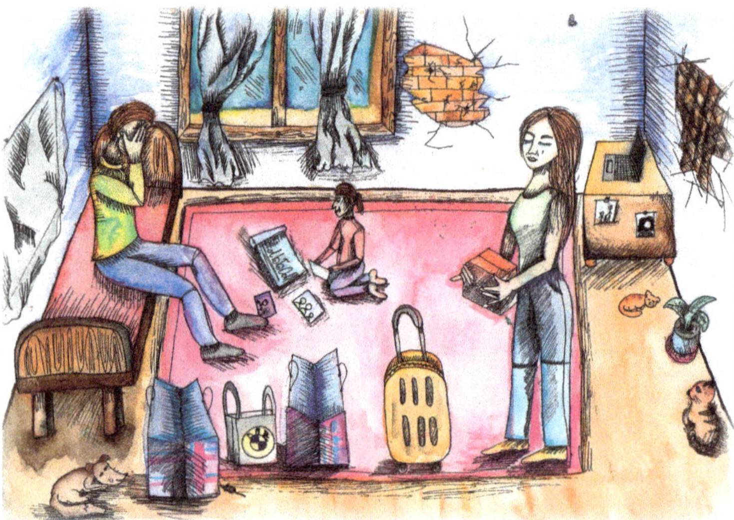

Khomyn Khrystyna, age14, ink and watercolor

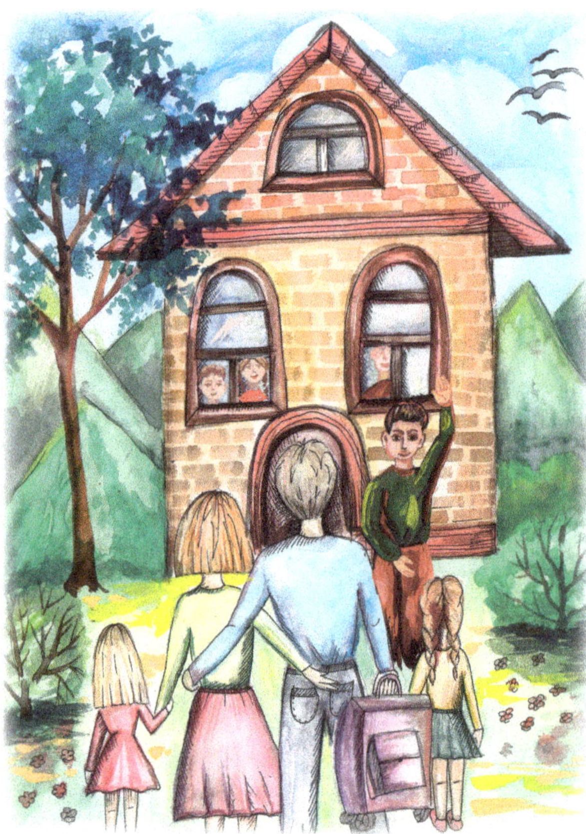

Polina Kasyan, age 13, A3 ink and watercolor

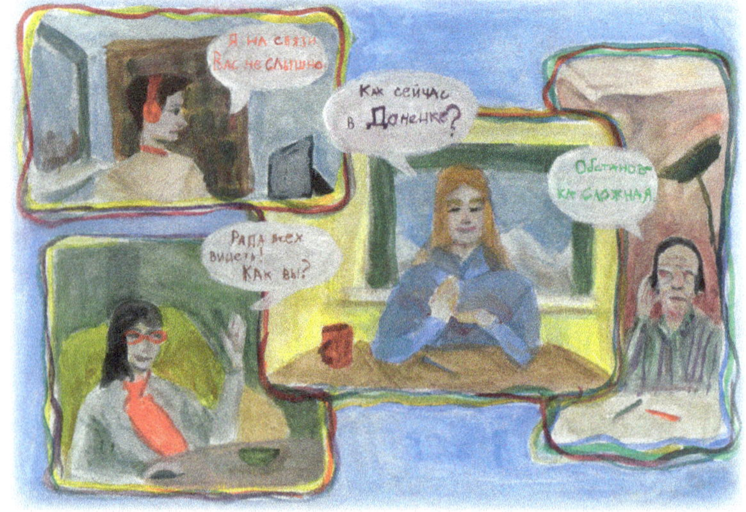

Maria Kycheryavays, age 16, A3 watercolor

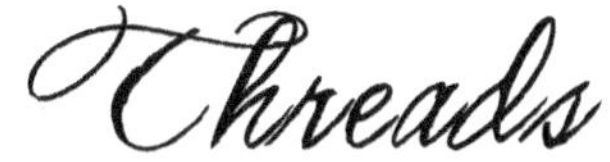

Threads

by Danilova Darya, Ukraine

"Life concentrates around the things into which we, against all the odds, continue to invest our efforts." Alexander Mokhovikov

As I fried potatoes on the stove, I called to my daughter, "Step aside from the window, they're shooting out there." My matter-of-fact tone surprised me.

Donetsk, once home to a million people, was now empty. When sounds of shooting and traffic stopped, the silence was oppressive. Exhausted by doubt, I asked my husband, "Should we run too, or stay?" Our world was fragile and unreliable, so we bought tickets and fled from Donetsk in May of 2014. "How could I pack a whole life into four bags? Would we ever return?" I wondered.

"Let's agree we're coming back," I suggested. "We can pack like we're going on holiday." That helped, but years later I wanted to go back to that evening and put the photo album in the bag. That day, however, I left it. It was heavy. And, we were coming back.

We shook in terror as we crossed the station square and boarded the train. Fear permeated the air and stifled our breathing. Only when we were out of the city did we exhale and breathe freely.

Our friends' welcomed us into a big house with three generations of their family. Our lovely hosts and their sense of safety and the blossoming gardens felt unreal, as I kept crying into my pillow. Our daughters asked, "Isn't it time to get back to school, so see our friends?" But time passed, and we all had to find ways to weave the threads of our lives back together.

My counseling practice was gone, but clients and colleagues began calling. We needed to connect as a group, so I took a deep breath and learned to use Skype.

Soon I opened an online counseling group. One after another, people I had known in Donetsk joined, "Where are you? How are you?" Many had scattered to Lviv, Kyiv, Zaporozhye, Odesa, the Transcarpathian Region, and even further to Belarus, Crimea, Israel, and Russia. Others had stayed in the war zones of Donetsk, Horlivka, or Makiivka. Sometimes, after a group session, I would sit for a moment trying to remember where I was.

In our group, the most loyal attendee was a counselor who had stayed in Donetsk. Sometimes we heard fighting, saw blasts fling his doors open, or he would suddenly lose internet connection. Once during a counseling session, as the blasts raged outside, he slid under his desk until the attack passed, then slid back up as if that were normal. Attending our group helped remind him that peace was alive, somewhere.

The group often pulled him out of despair, back to hope. This took some extra attention, but our care for him and each other became the binding threads weaving our lives back together. We came from different ideological and political views, and although war magnifies such differences, we would not let it divide us. We kept in touch, searched for others, and kept track of each others' travels. In this reliable, safe space, we could smile and learn to take joy in life.

The years passed, and we never went home. We rented a house, and got a dog, a cat, and a parrot. Even the children got used to their new school and came to truly love the new landscape, but they still dreamt of Donetsk. My heart became filled with gratitude and respect for all the people who continue to be the threads that weave the fabric of our lives.

Part 3: Reaching Out to Each Other

Stories from Chechnya, Russia, Ukraine, and USA

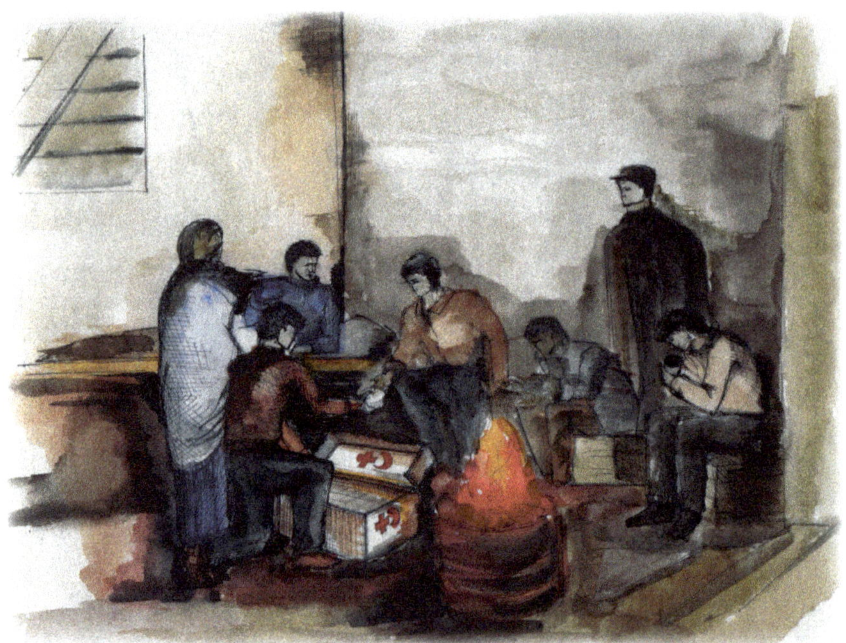

Alicia Homichenko, age 16, lost original, watercoler

> "Chechen children bear bloodstained inscriptions cut deep into their hearts by war, suffering and want.
> The suffering of Chechnya's children is great indeed, so great that if they could express it, their bitter tears would cover the whole of the planet."
>
> ~ Musa Akhmadov, Chechen writer

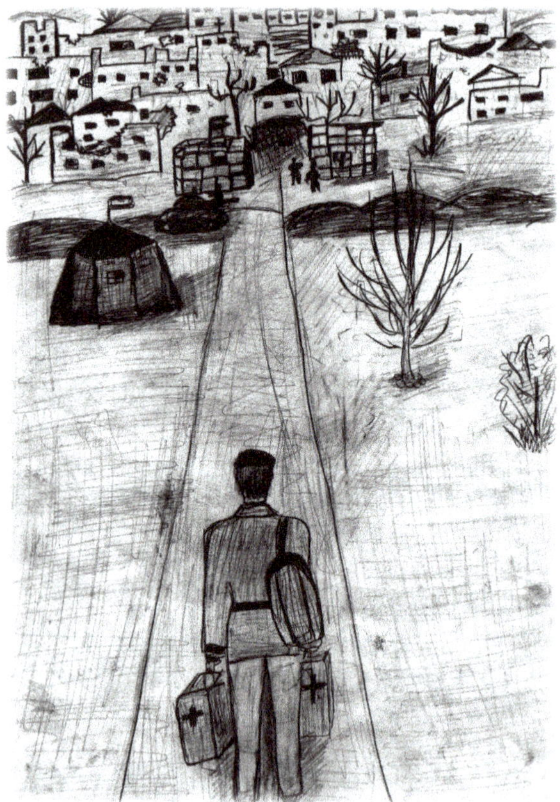

Marina Kurbanova, age 14, 11.25 x 8 in. pencil

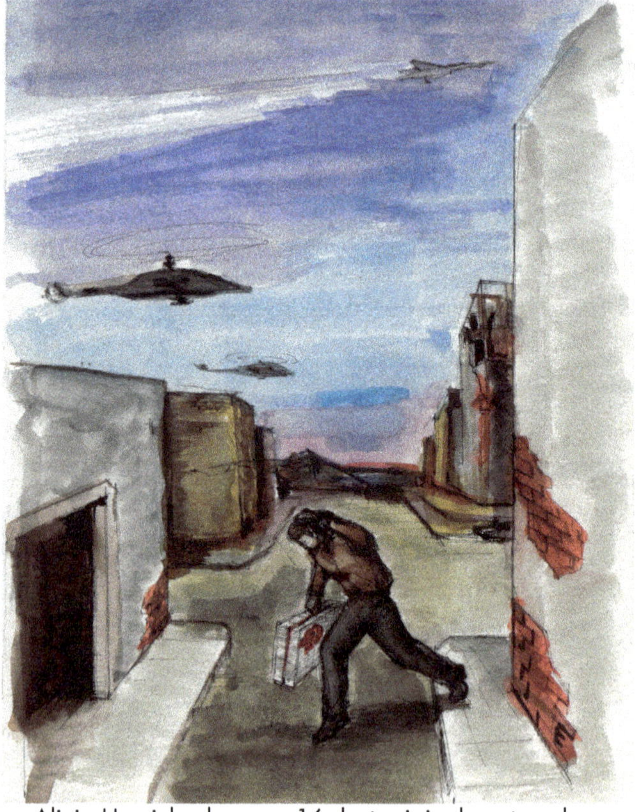

Alicia Homichenko, age 16, lost original, watercolor

Allah is Merciful: Perhaps Allah Needs Me

by Patricia Cockrell, Chechnya

Everyone liked Shaman, and he liked everyone and everything. He lived in the Muslim village of Sernovodsk in Chechnya in a green valley with small farms. The people lived a good life, and were proud of their school, agricultural college and hot sulfur baths. Shaman worked in a bakery, but he liked mechanics, electronics, construction, Beethoven… even rock music. He could mend practically anything, from cars to sewing machines.

When he was 24, he left his family, job, friends and hobbies for Moscow to earn money for his parents and younger brothers. Before long, however, war broke out in Chechnya. Shaman took the first plane home. He sat next to foreign journalists on the plane. Shaman accepted their offer of 1,000 U.S. dollars to be their driver and guide in Grozny, the capitol of Chechnya.

There, Shaman found a world of bombs, dead bodies, ruined buildings, shattered glass, broken furniture, and belongings scattered everywhere. To his surprise, people still lived in the basements amidst this horror. Most were Russians, but some were Chechens, Azeris, or others. They all huddled together, terrified and helpless, without food, water, heat or light.

Shaman promised, Allah willing, to bring them food, water and medicine. He kept his promise again and again. Running and dodging on back streets, Shaman and his brother Adlan avoided snipers to take in supplies that he had bought, and bring out the sick and wounded.

"Allah is merciful," he told himself. "Perhaps Allah needs me."

When his own village became blockaded, he walked 43 kilometers (nearly 27 miles) over mountains to take food and medicine to survivors in another village. He even brought food to Russian soldiers, who had attacked the Chechens, because they were hungry and cold. To Shaman no one in need was an enemy.

Meanwhile, Shaman's neighbors refused to let war take over. They set up a peace camp on the main road to speak to passersby and pray around a campfire in a makeshift mosque. People stayed in the peace camp all winter, but in the spring thousands, including Shaman's family, fled new bombings. Luckily, Shaman and his family were taken in by friends in neighboring Ingushetia.

Shaman knew that neither the Chechens nor his Russian friends wanted war. He looked forward to returning home to raise a family of his own, in peace. Finally, that time came. The fighting stopped. Shaman, Adlan, and the rest of their family and friends returned to Sernovodsk. They found much destroyed, but worked hard to rebuild.

Best of all, Shaman met and married Milana. Their baby girl, Diana, was born on Christmas day. They rebuilt more than a home. With the help of a young British Quaker, Chris, and others from many cultures, they set up a mill to grind 50 sacks of flour a day for people in need. Meanwhile, Adlan and Chris opened a center in Grozny called Little Star to help children, who were hurt by the war, to laugh and play as children should.

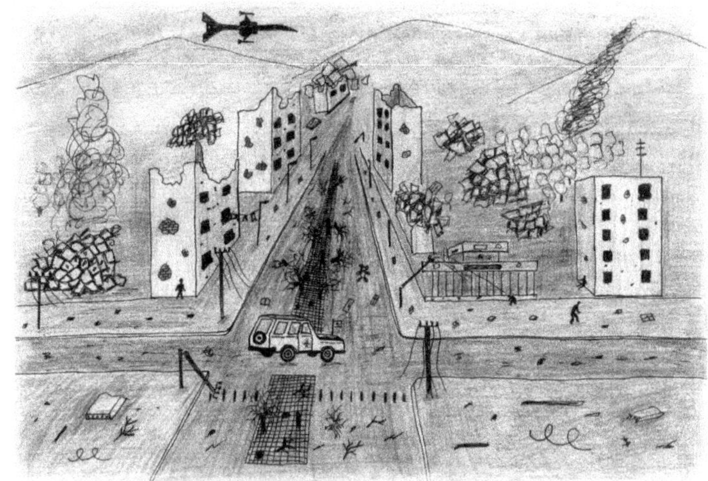

Unknown, 11.5 x 8.25 in. pencil

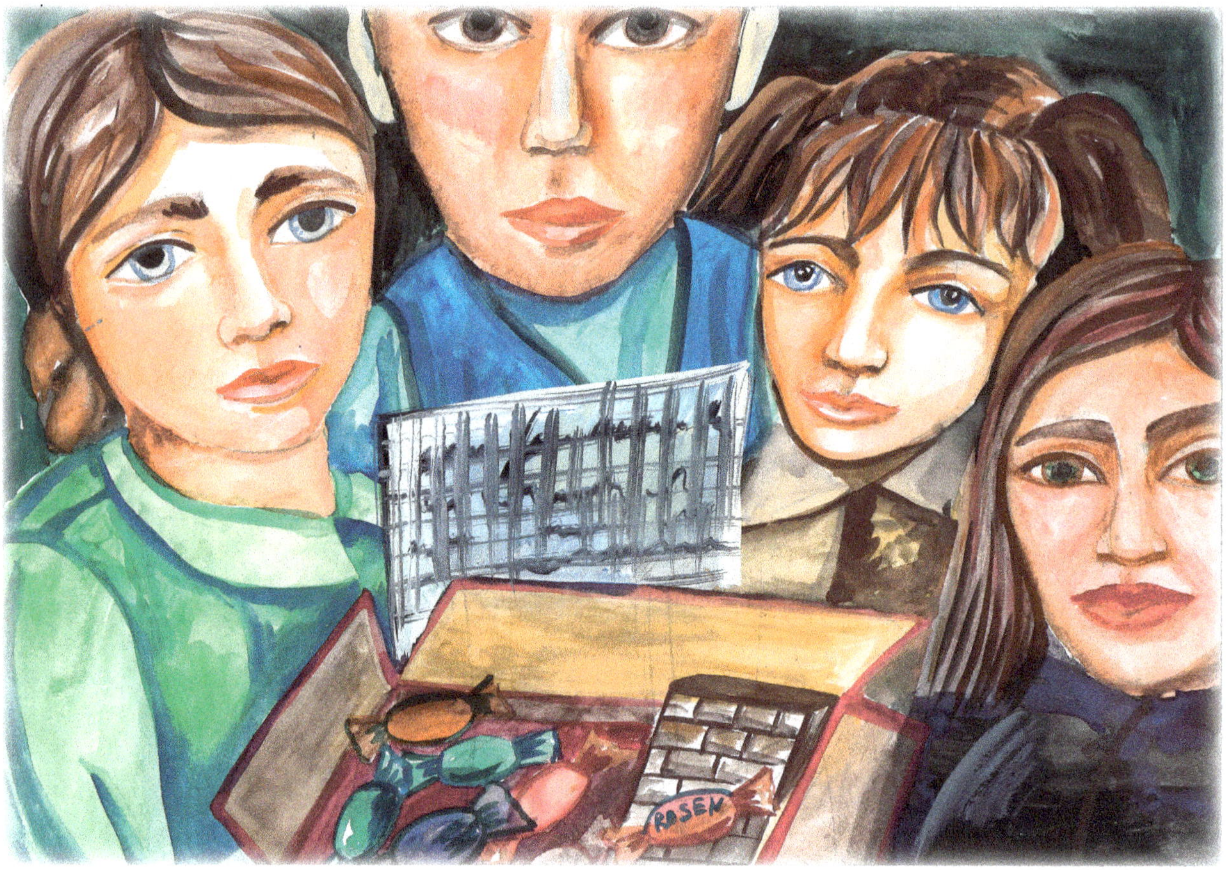

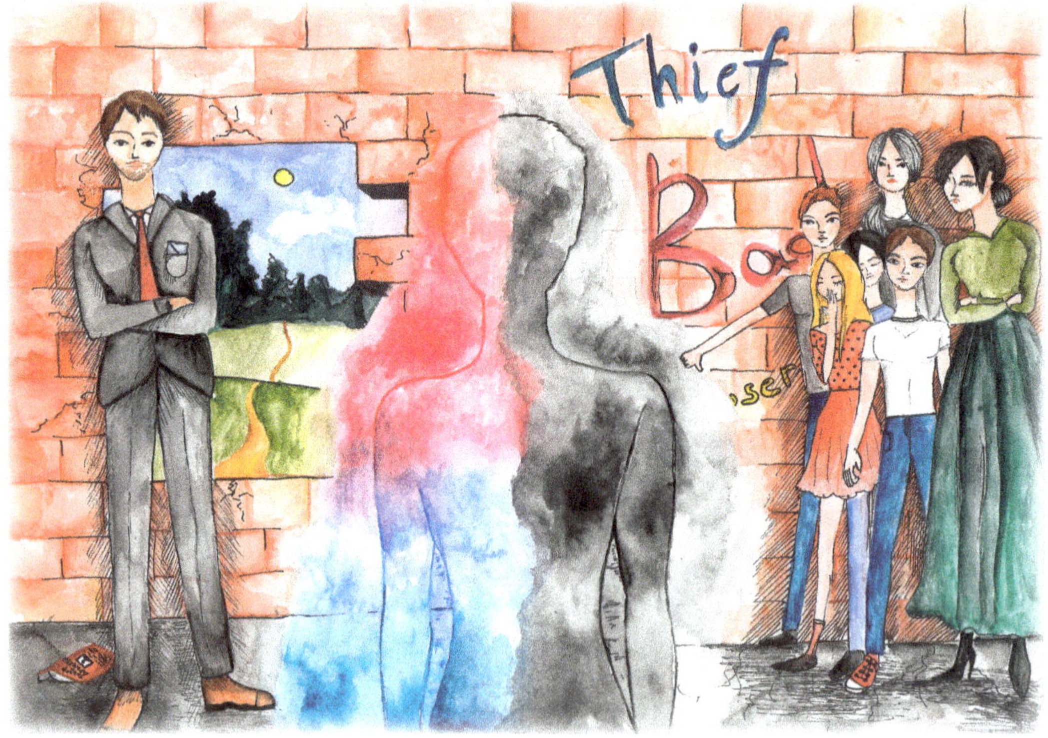

Anastasija Pogorelova, age 13, tempera

Yanytska Yuliana, age 13, ink and watercolor

Brick

by Alexander Matsulevich, Ukraine

Whether because of his surname or his constant scruffiness, scratches and cuts, nobody knew exactly why, but the other boys in the village school called him Brick. He had no father. When his mother came to school, if at all, she appeared unkempt and often confused.

Most of the teachers had a low opinion of Brick. They pointed out that he had been smoking since the third grade, and often fought with the other boys. They accused him of stealing, and often blamed him for all sorts of trouble.

One teacher, though, saw him differently. He noticed that Brick loved to read. After class, Brick told the teacher he had read Tom Sawyer seven times – nobody else had read it even once. He was eager to read *Don Quixote*, also, but the library wouldn't lend it to him. An excerpt from *The Toreadors from Vasyukovka* had been in their textbook, and Brick wanted to read the whole book. With some hesitation, the teacher lent him his personal copy. After reading it, Brick returned it in perfect condition.

The class read a letter by Umberto Eco to his grandson in which he said it was important, at any age, to train one's memory by memorizing a poem a week. The teacher suggested the class take up this challenge, but only Brick did so, and without embarrassment recited a poem in front of the whole class.

The teacher moved away. Then one day, on Facebook, he learned that Brick had been removed from the village and sent to a children's home. The teacher contacted the home to see how Brick was getting along. He learned that Brick had run away from the home twice. He had actually made it back to the village, only to find nobody who wanted him.

The teacher decided to visit him at the children's home. Knowing Brick's curious nature, the teacher brought Brick a book, *The Financier* by Theodore Dreiser. He told Brick it would help him learn about making money, which could be very useful in the future. He encouraged Brick to stop running away, so he could study hard and go to college. Then he could learn a trade, and go back to the village if he wanted. The teacher did not promise to come back. He didn't like making promises he wasn't certain he could keep. Brick didn't need that anyway.

When the teacher contacted the old village school, he told the class about Brick. It was almost New Year's, so the students put together a package of sweets to send to Brick. One of the boys wrote a letter on a page torn from an exercise book, "How are you doing, Brick? When are you coming back? Give us a call if you need anything," and included a mobile phone number.

Brick had thought nobody cared about him. With the encouragement of his former teacher and classmates, Brick gained a renewed sense of enthusiasm. He worked hard and was accepted into college. After he graduated, he moved back home to the village. He had earned his name – he was as strong, sturdy, and reliable as a brick.

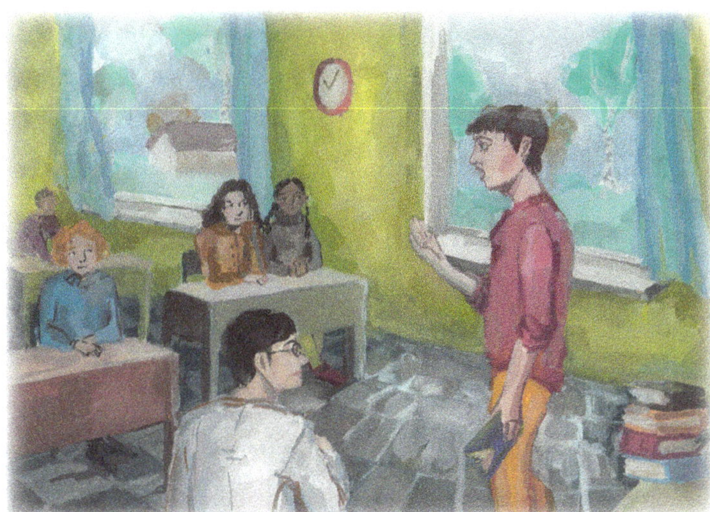

Anastasija Pogorelova, age 16, watercolor

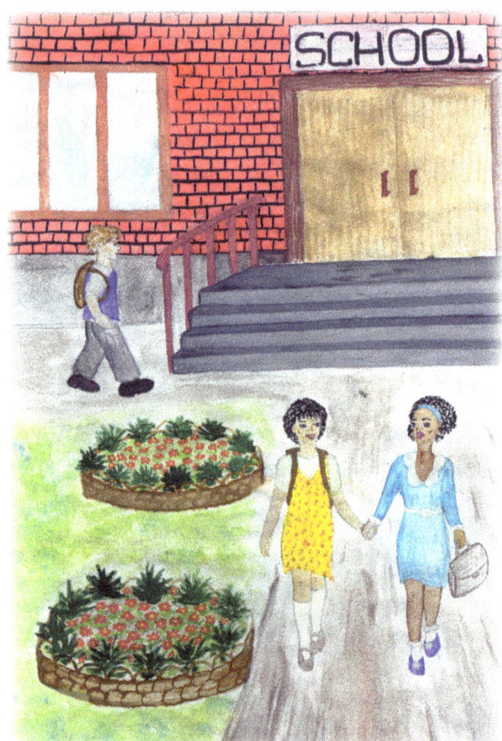

Anzor Hashagulov, 8 x 11.5 in. watercolor

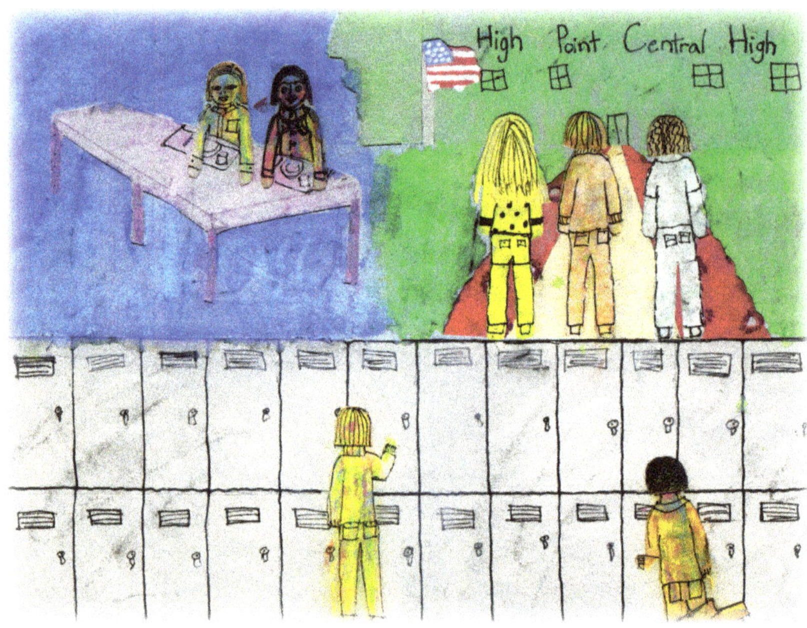

Saskia Hanover, age 12, 12 x 9 in. ink, construction paper and watercolor

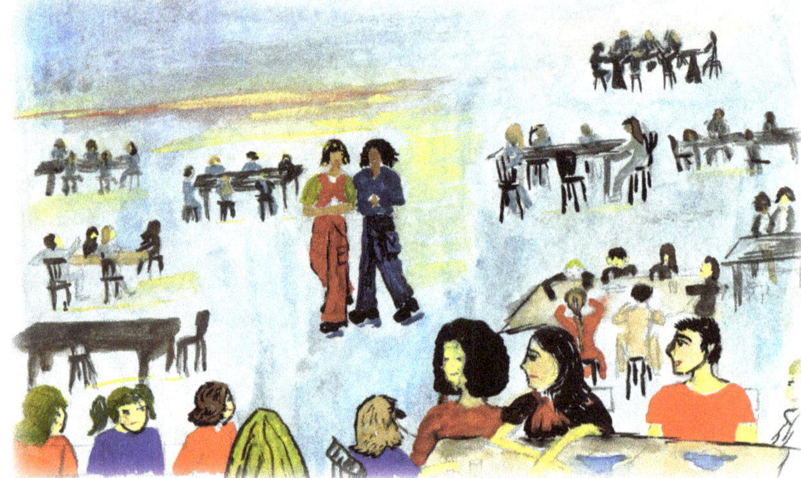

Malika Saieva, age 19, 11.75 x 8.25 in. ink and watercolor

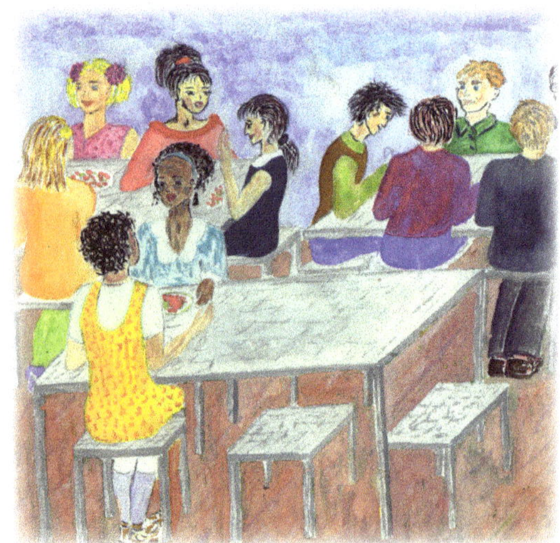

Anzor Hashagulov, 7.75 x 7.5 in. watercolor

New Girl in School

by Carol Passmore, United States of America

"So," said Annette, "we decided to be nice to her."

"Who?" I asked.

Annette called the new girl by an awful name. "The principal says we aren't to have trouble like in other schools."

Lib giggled. "Then better not call her that."

"Sure," I said. "We should be nice." I hadn't thought about it. Besides, it was a big school; I'd probably never see her.

I was wrong. Her name was Lynn, and she was in my algebra class, sitting quietly in the back. And in my English class, quietly in front. In history, she sat right by me.

I decided to show Lynn the cafeteria. I wondered if that was "too nice," but remembered my first lunch, alone, the year before.

There was a long cafeteria line. Everyone got quiet when we joined it. After we got our food, tables were getting full. We sat at a half-empty table with kids I didn't know. They all got up and left, and no one would join us.

We stared at each other. Her short black hair was wavy, her skin a rich coppery brown. My brown hair was short and wavy and my tanned skin almost as brown as hers. I figured we could pass as sisters.

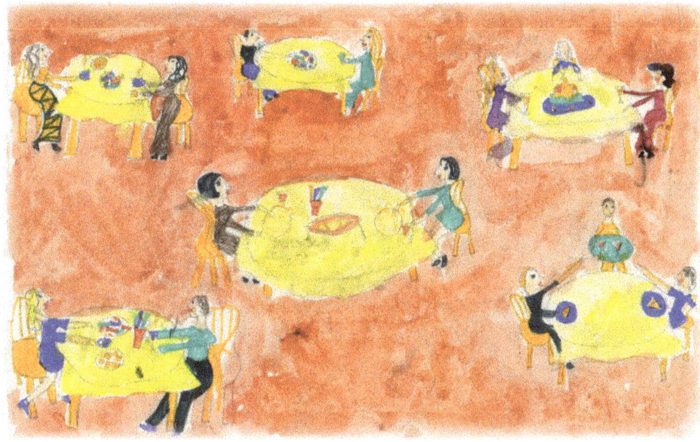

Unknown, 11.5 x 8 in. watercolor

"If they don't want to eat with us," I muttered, "I'm not sure they're my friends."

So I stayed, and through junior and senior years, Lynn and I ate together. We had a private table; no one ever had the courage to join us.

A good thing was, my friends and a lot of other kids were polite to Lynn. The bad part was, they were polite to me too. Lib explained "When we said friendly, we didn't mean that friendly."

Some kids called us names and threw things, but nothing serious. No one didn't know us. Over time Lynn and I discovered we had lots in common. Besides almost all the same classes, we had the same interests.

The best thing about those years was meeting people with the American Friends Service Committee, who taught Lynn and me about nonviolence and helped us be nice to people who called us names. They introduced us to others who didn't think your color should determine where you went to school or what job you could have. We had fun with them, which made up for not being in many high school activities.

Sometimes I look at my school yearbooks. Sophomore year, when I worked so hard at being popular, lots of kids signed my book, saying how nice I was. Junior year only a few signed, and wrote nothing personal. My senior yearbook was different. All those kids I had wanted as friends signed it. They wrote how they admired someone standing up for her beliefs. They didn't say they changed their minds about race relations, and I'm not sure being admired made up for being lonely and left out, but I was glad they were willing to sign.

The best was from Lynn, who wrote a whole page. She wrote how scared she was that first day, and how glad she was when I spoke to her. I was surprised; she never looked scared. But then, you can't know everything about your best friend.

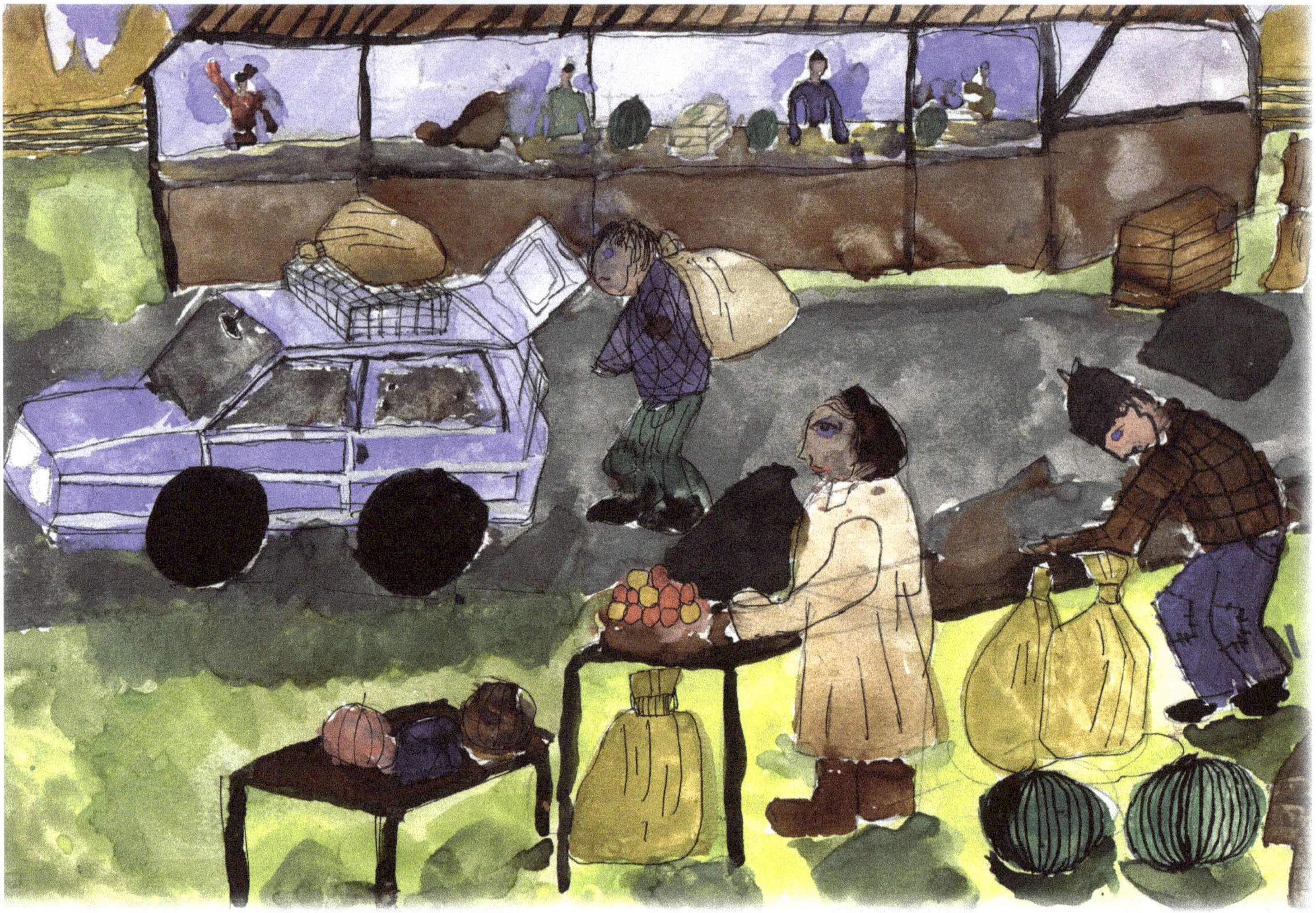

Gleb Komarov, age 9, 16.5 x 11.75 in. ink and watercolor

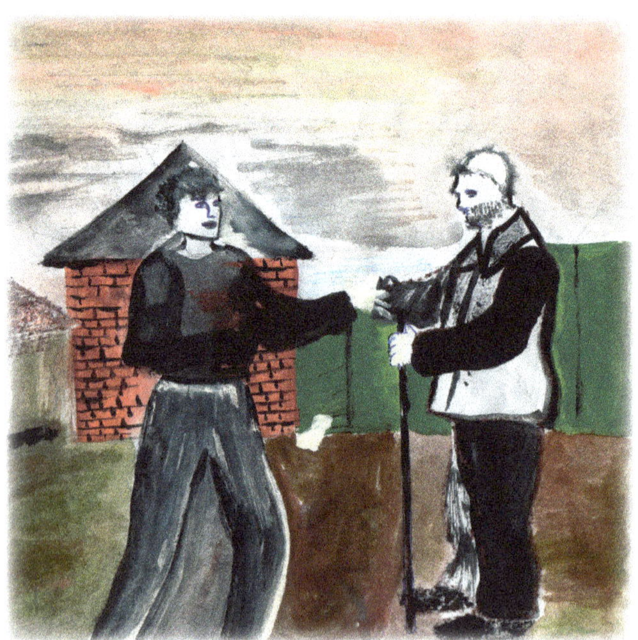

Asya Umarova, age 16, 11 x 8.25 in. ink

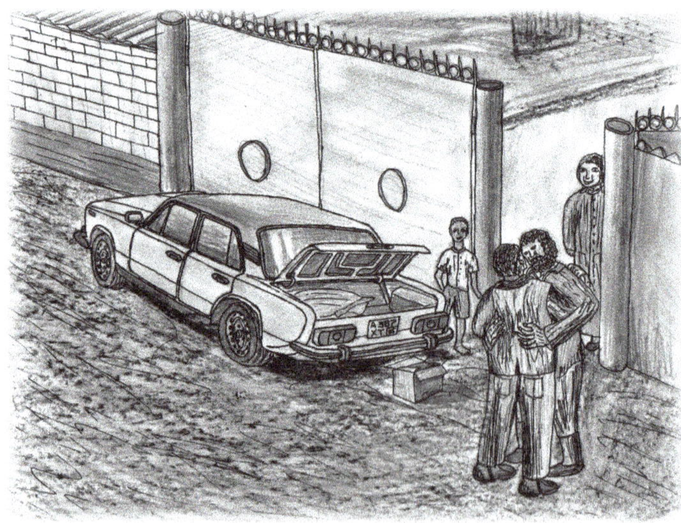

Asya Umarova, age 16, 10 x 8 in. pencil and ink

Reunion

by Zalpa Bersanova from *Autobiography*, Chechnya

Alexey knew the man in the photo on his mother's dresser was his father. Where was he? What had happened to him? Mother would never say.

Alexey grew up and joined the Russian army. When he got orders to go to Chechnya, his mother finally talked about his father. "He's Chechen," she said. "We were too different to be happy together, so he went home to Chechnya. I hope he has married again and is happy. I did not want you to know about him, though he sent money to help take care of you here in Moscow. Be sure to find him. Help him. Things aren't easy." That was all. She gave him an address.

Alexey had no trouble finding the little brick house where his father lived. He drove up in an armored car. A little nervous, he knocked on the door. He was hoping for a joyful reunion, but the woman who answered his knock was terrified. Several badly dressed children hid behind her.

"So these are my brothers and sisters," thought Alexey. "Where's father?" he asked.

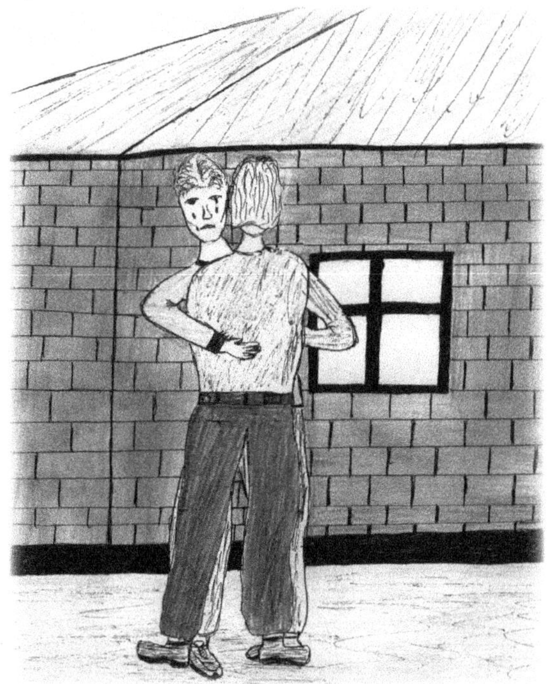

Zhabrel Alhanov, age unknown 8.25 x 11.75 in. ink and pencil

"He's not here," the woman replied in broken Russian. "He left long ago. I don't know where he went." The children all backed up their mother, nodding their heads. They stared at Alexey like frightened wolf cubs.

Alexey thought, "They must have decided that I had come to take him away like Russian soldiers take other Chechen men without notice. They think I am trying to trick them. They will never tell me where he is."

The next day, Alexey drove to the house again, hoping to bump into his father by accident. The gates were closed. The same woman answered his knock with the same youngsters. Again, they refused to say where his father was.

Alexey sighed and drove away. Plainly, fate had decided that he and his father should remain strangers. His tour of duty was nearly over. But his mother's words came back to him, "Be sure to find your father and help him."

Next morning, Alexey got up early. He drove to the market and bought sweets for the children and sacks of flour and sugar for their mother. He loaded them into a small rented car. Then he dressed in civilian clothes and drove to the house.

The reception was much friendlier. He was glad to see the children's eyes light up as he offered them the sweets. The oldest boy helped Alexey unload the sacks from the car.

The woman said something to the youngest child, who rushed away toward the house. Soon, an older man came out into the yard. He looked intently at the visitor, then came forward to meet him. Alexey wiped the sweat from his forehead and looked up. He saw a face with a broad smile, the same face in the photo on his mother's dresser.

"Hello, Father," Alexey said. It was a perfect moment, one he had waited for as long as he could remember.

"The practices of goodness—noticing, savoring, thinking, enjoying and being thankful— are not hard disciplines to learn. But they are disciplines, and they take practice. The habits that allow wrong to become entrenched— mindlessness, tuning out, inattentiveness, the busyness of doing to distraction, and the ungrateful heart— can take hold so easily."
~ Desmond and Mpho Tutu,
Made for Goodness

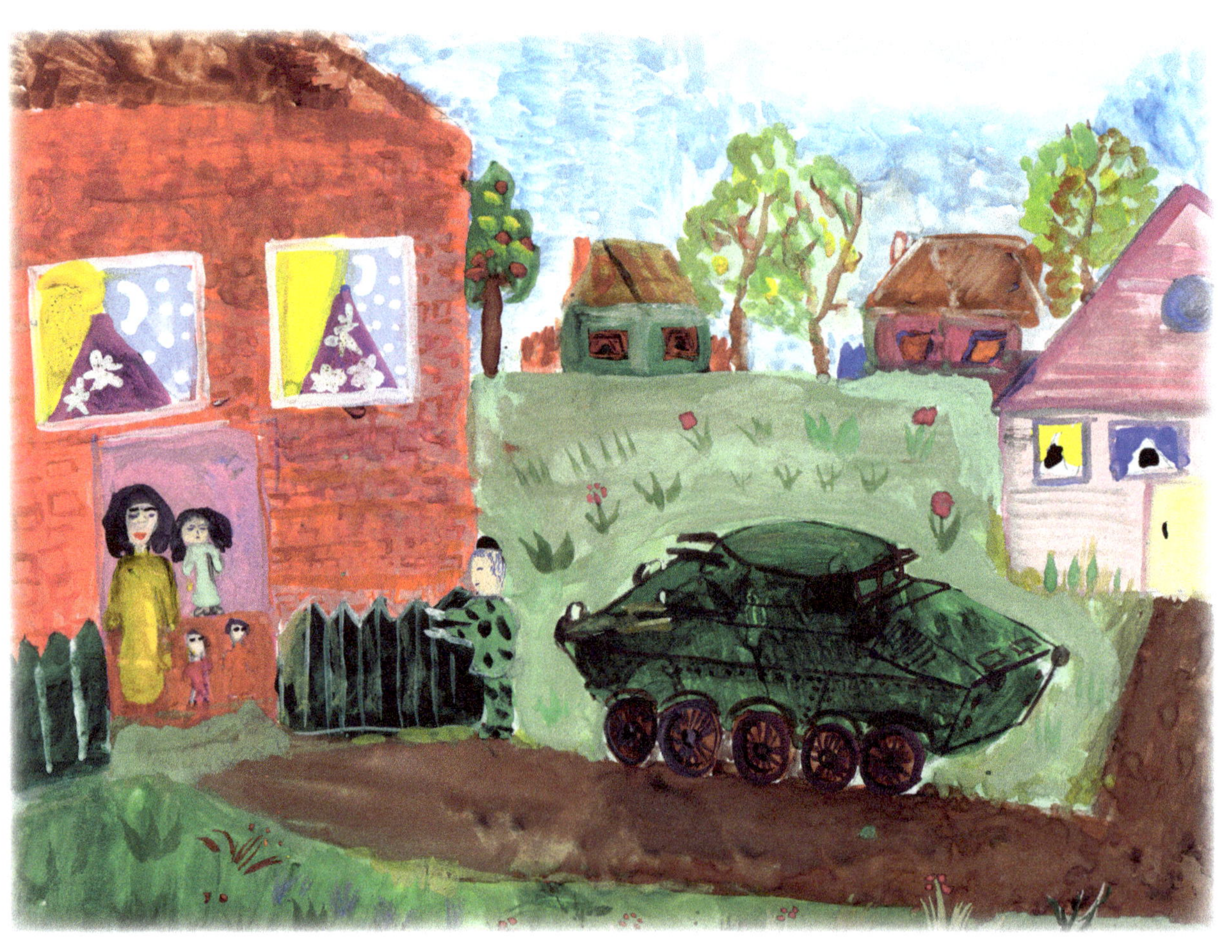

Masha Romanenko, age 10, 16 x 13 in. tempera

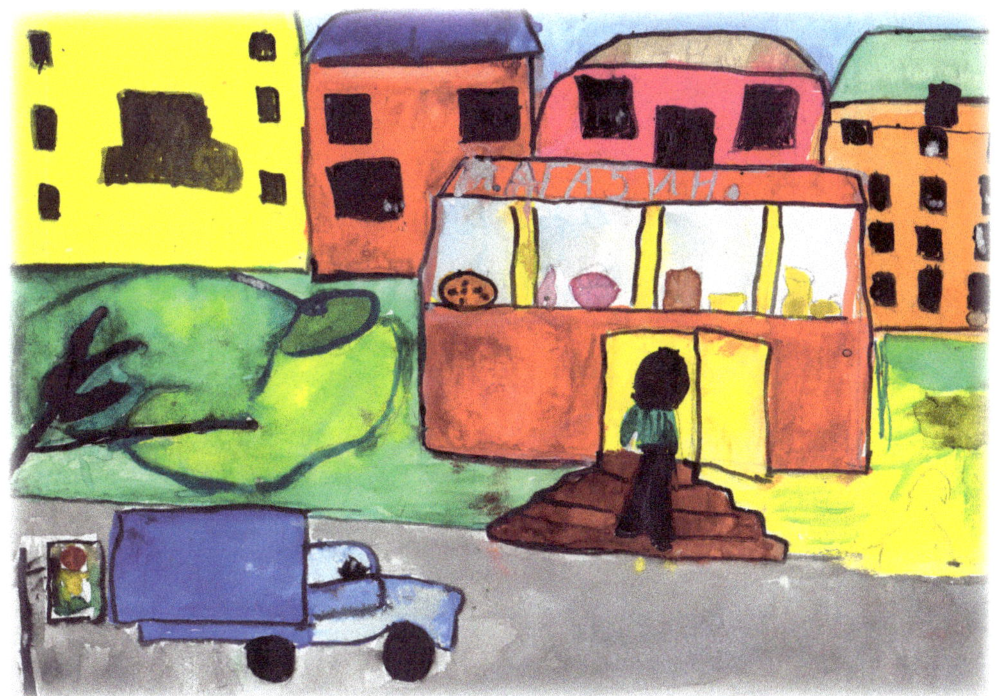

Milana Kurbanov, age 11, 11 x 9 in. watercolor

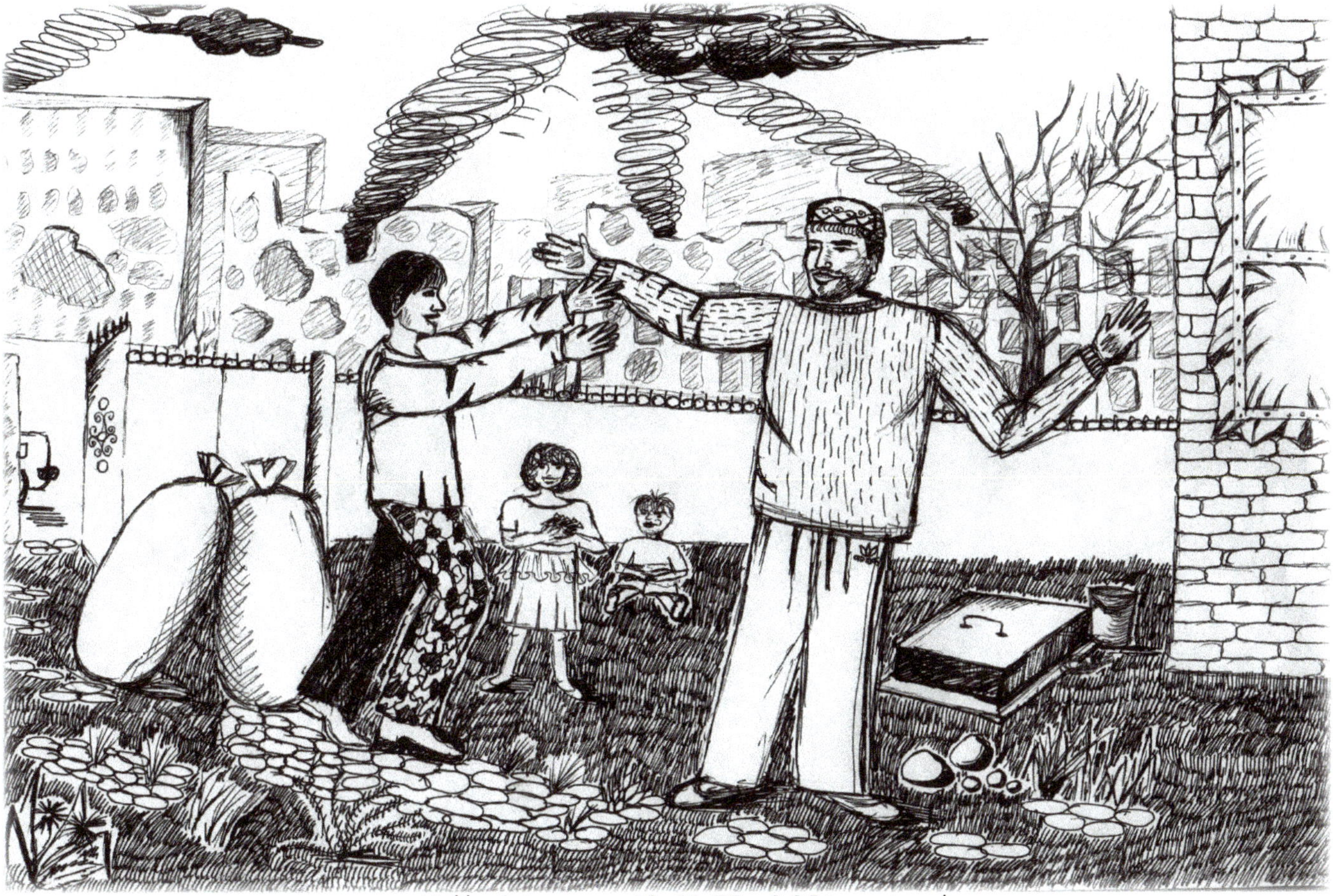

Malika Saieva, age 19, 11.75 x 8.25 in. watercolor

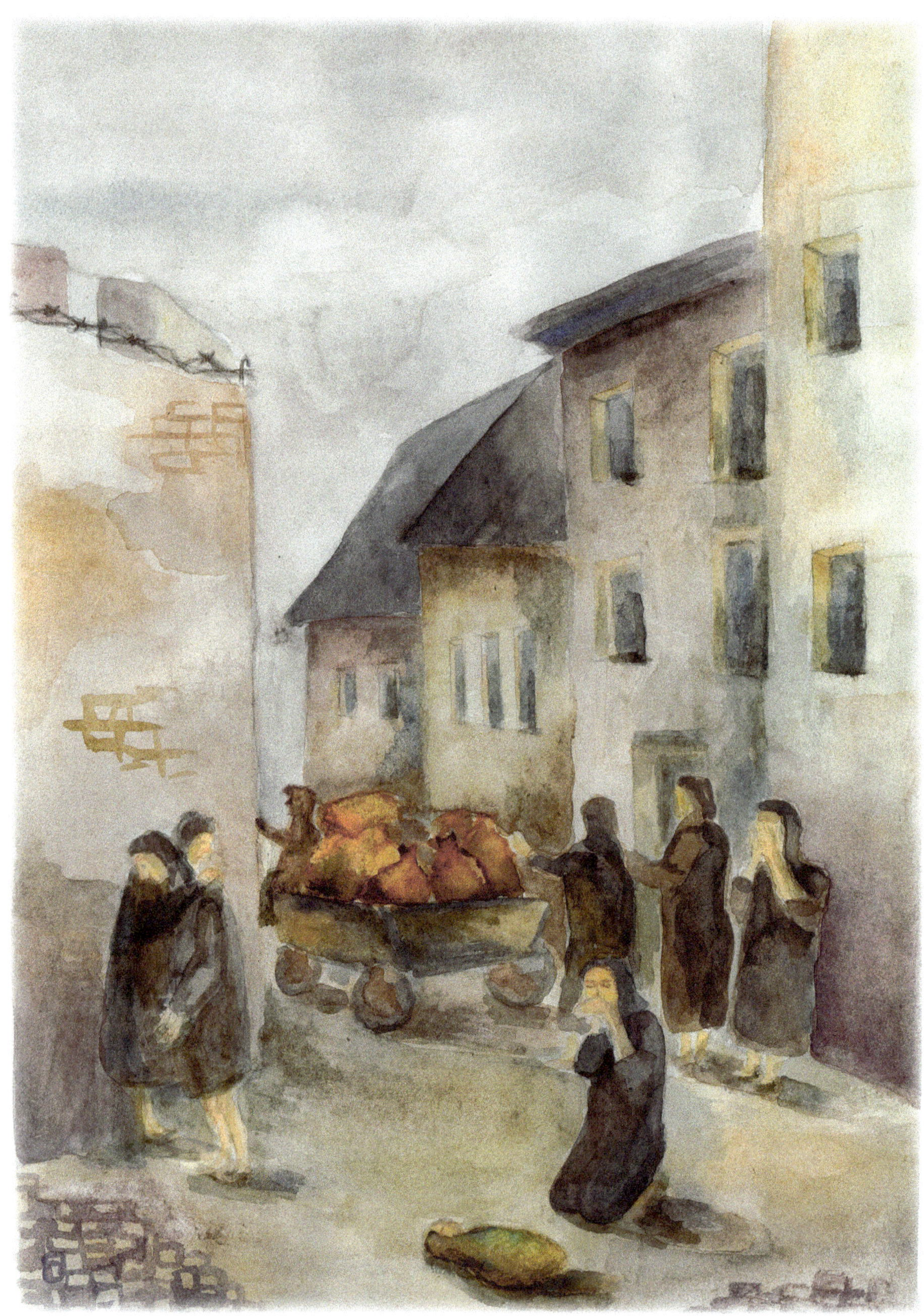

Maria Navolotskaya, age 19, A3 watercolor

Sacks of Potatoes

by Konstantin Georgievich Paustovsky, from *Beginning of an Unknown Era*, Ukraine

Recently an acquaintance told me a surprising story. Soon after the war, travelling by train, an old man sat opposite him in the carriage and told him this story.

Listen, I live on the outskirts of Riga, the capital city of Latvia. Right before the war, a man settled near my house. He was a dishonest and cruel man, a speculator and profiteer; he had no heart and no honor. Some people say speculation is just making money, but it's greedy when it's made at the expense of human grief and children's tears.

Well, one day the Germans occupied Riga and herded all the Jewish people into the ghetto. The ghetto was blocked off. They shot anyone who approached within fifty steps. Hundreds of Jews were dying every day, especially children. So my greedy neighbour got the good idea to load a wagon with potatoes, bribe the German security man to let him into the ghetto, and exchange potatoes for jewelry. Rumor was that the Jewish people in the ghetto still had a lot of jewelry.

I saw him in the street before he left. "I will deal only with women who have children," he bragged. "They will do anything for their children's sake, so I can make three times more money." The blood rushed to my fists. If he had not left at once, I might have killed him in my rage.

He went to load his wagon with sacks of potatoes and go to the ghetto. He bribed the warden, who said, "They have nothing left but their empty stomachs. You will have to take your rotten potatoes back home; I would bet on it."

In the ghetto, he went into the courtyard of a big house. Women and children circled his wagon. Suddenly, he didn't know how it happened, he was tearing the ties off the sacks and spilling the potatoes out on the ground. "Hurry!" he cried to the women. "Give me the children. I'll take them out of here. Let them only stay motionless and quiet. Hurry!"

Mothers began to put their children into the sacks. They knew they would never see them again, but they did not even take the time to kiss them good-bye. He loaded his wagon with children hidden in the sacks, left a couple of sacks of potatoes on each side of the wagon, and drove away without a backward glance. He clucked at his horse loudly, afraid that one of the children could start to cry and give them all away. But the children kept quiet.

The warden saw him and shouted, "Didn't I tell you that you were a fool? Get out with your stinking potatoes before the lieutenant comes." He drove by the warden, cursing. He drove along wild country roads to the forest where partisans lived. He left the children with them. He told his wife that the Germans had taken his potatoes. But when the war was over, he left Riga.

The old Latvian on the train was silent for a while. "Now I think," he said, and smiled for the first time, "that it would have been terrible if I had lost my temper and killed him with my fists."

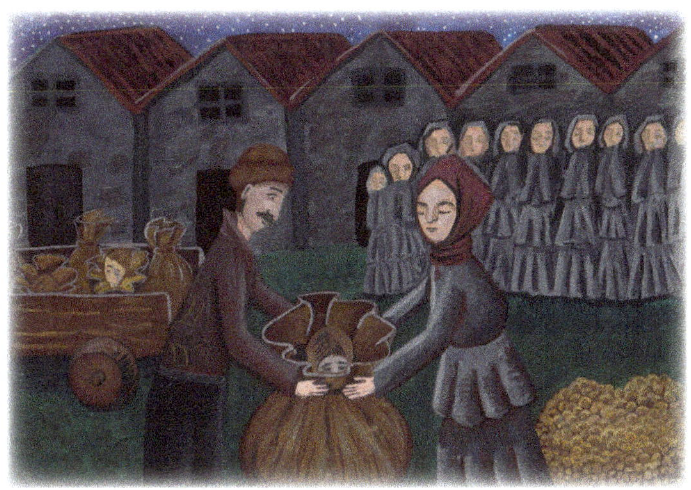

Anita Luytanicha, age 15. A3 tempera

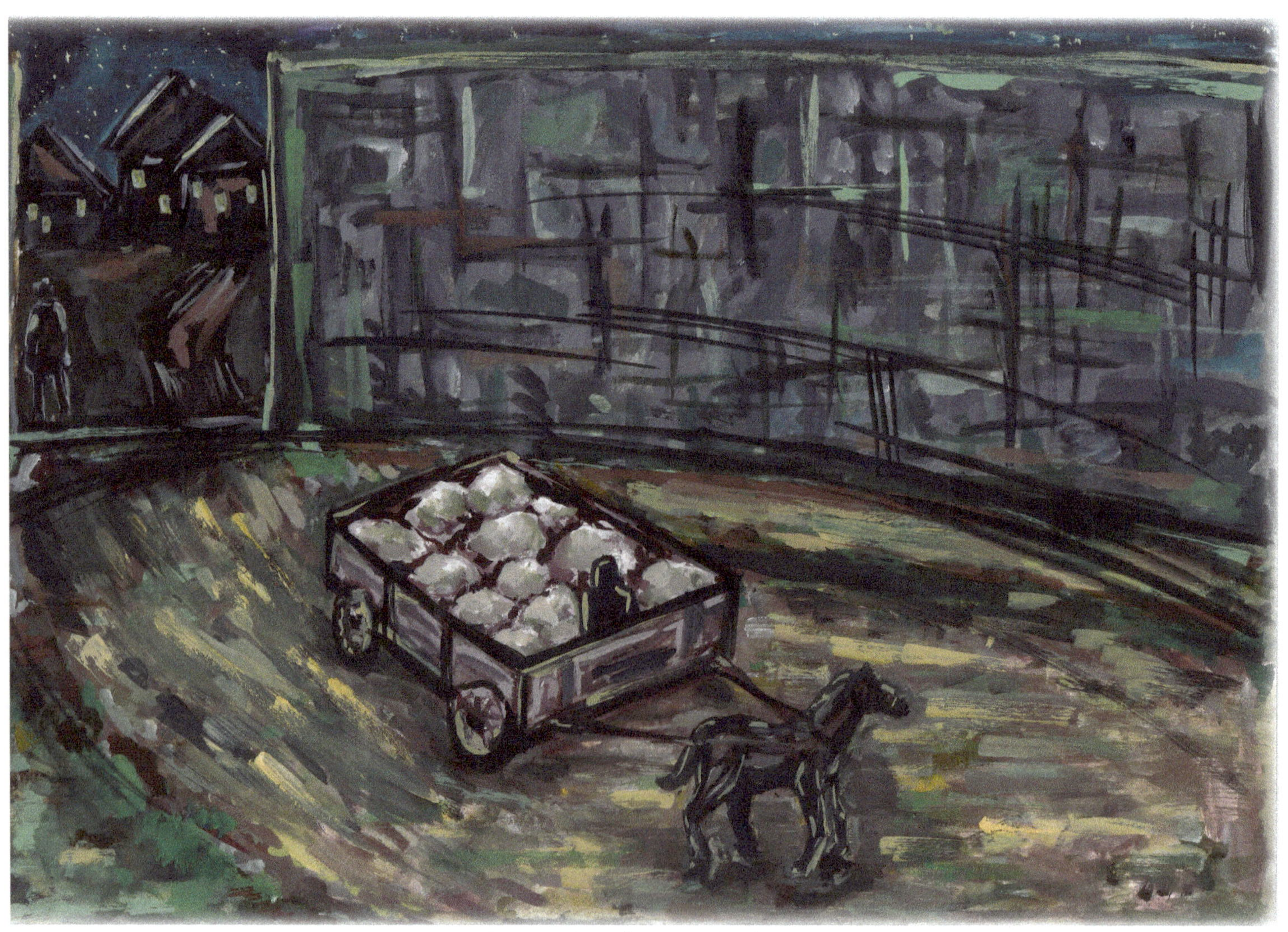

Daryna Manoylo, age 14, A3 tempera

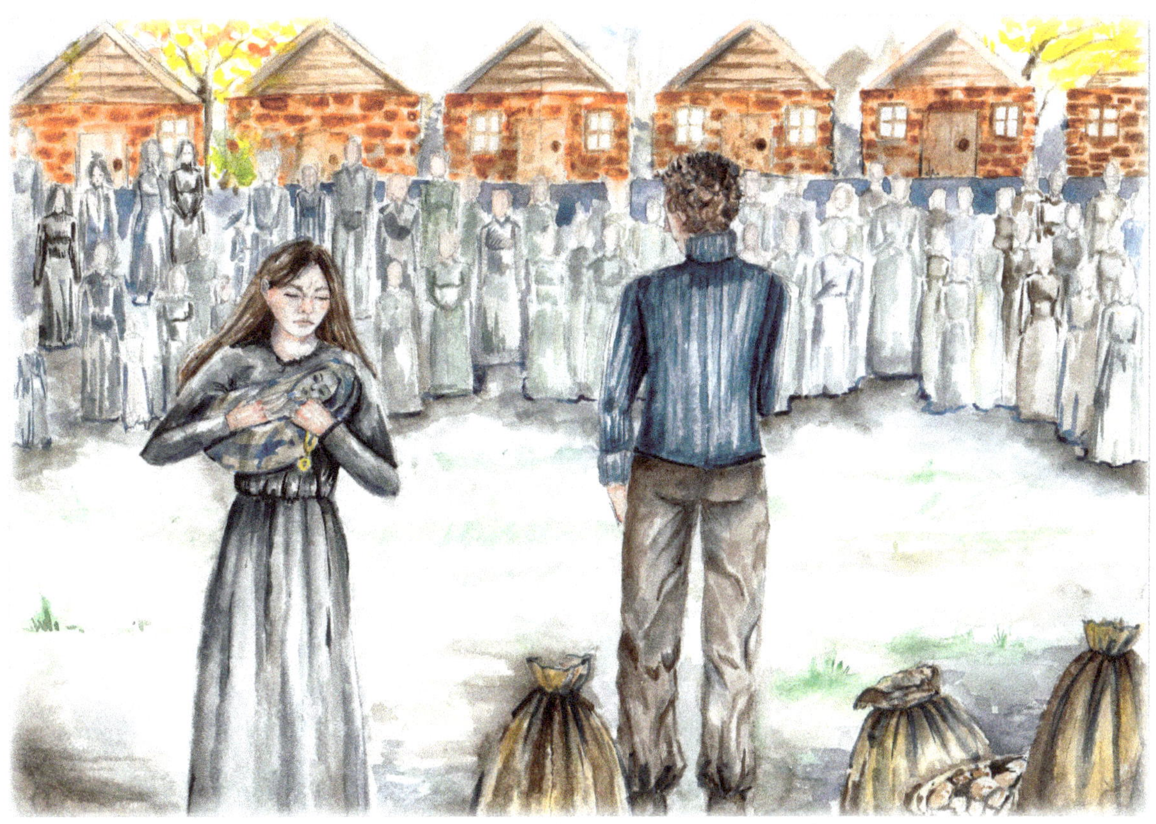

Anastasia Krasovska, age 14, A3 watercolor

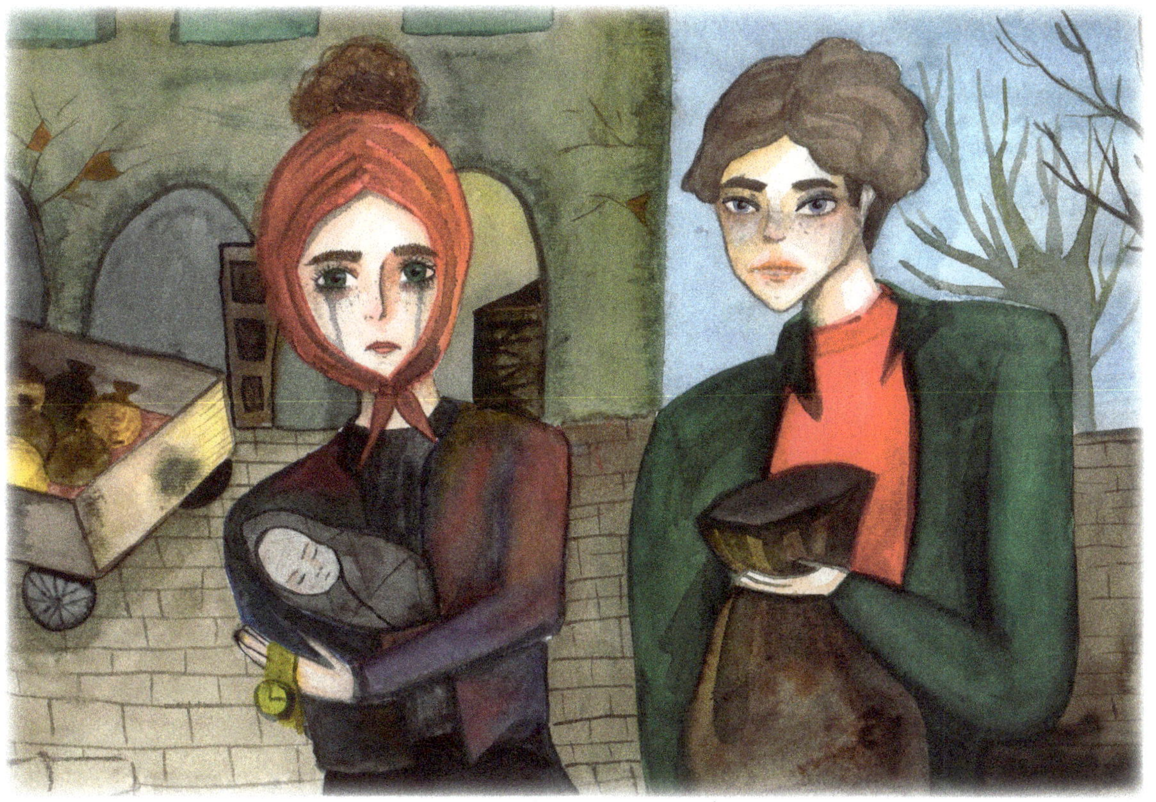

Anna Voitovich, age 15, A3 tempera

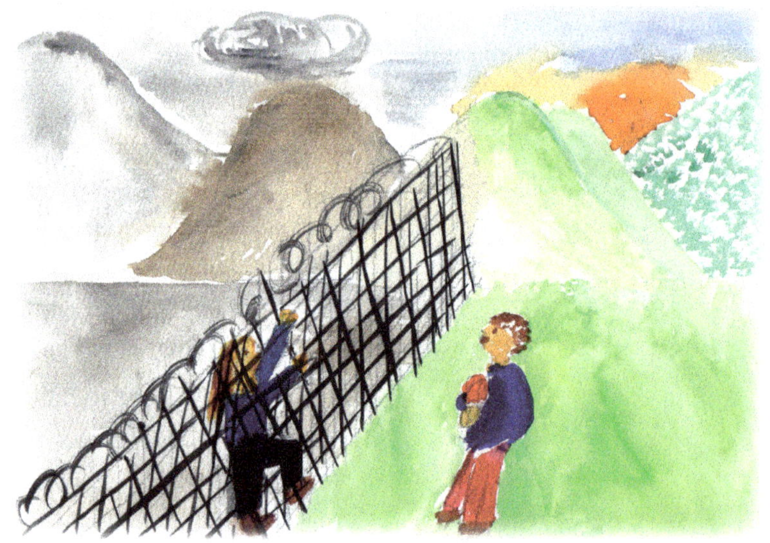

Lisa Engelhardt,
age 14, watercolor

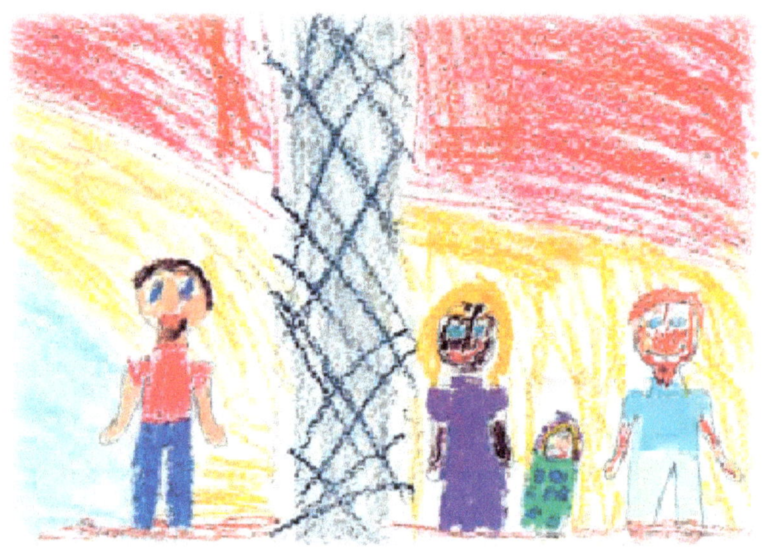

Unknown, age 7,
11 x 8.5 in. crayon

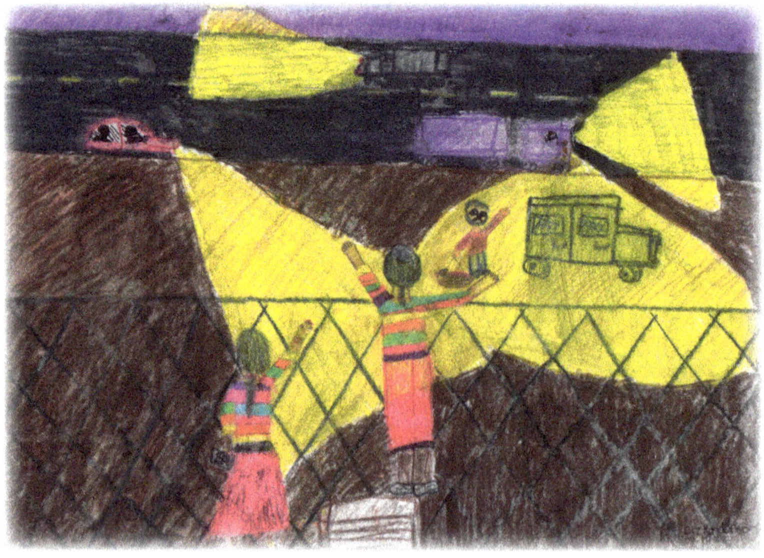

Elizabeth Henderson,
age 11, 11.75 x 8.75
in. colored pencil

Sanctuary Means Love

by Elizabeth Yeats, United States of America

The call came late one night. "Can you give sanctuary to two young families fleeing Guatemala? They're stranded in Mexico. We're worried they aren't getting enough to eat. Someone must help them across the border."

Our Quaker meeting knew of the violence in Central America and the thousands fleeing from arrest and torture by their own governments. We slept in warm, comfortable beds and woke feeling safe each morning. We wanted to share this security with the refugees, as others were doing.

"We might break our government's laws, but we would follow God's law to help people in trouble," one friend commented. "We are few, and we aren't rich, but doesn't God call us to share what we have?" asked another. An older woman reasoned, "If God means us to do this, the way will open. I think we should go ahead." We became a Sanctuary.

When the call came, I wondered if we were ready to care for two families. Who would travel thousands of miles to the border to help them cross? Real human beings needed our help; would the way really open?

In the morning the group asked my husband John to go. He spoke fluent Spanish and had worked with refugees. I waited to hear everyone was safe.

Border police arrested, tried, and fined or imprisoned U.S. citizens helping people cross the border illegally. John knew his family and the Quakers would help him. The danger for the refugees was far greater. If caught, border police would detain and deport them. Carlos was arrested four times for speaking against the government, and narrowly escaped being killed. If they sent him back, they would kill him. Then what would happen to his young wife Maria and their baby Anna?

John called to say that everyone had crossed safely.

In Mexico food had been scarce, so Anna and Maria grew too weak to travel. As a Guatemalan, Carlos could not work. So Mexicans in the Sanctuary Movement found them food and shelter until they grew strong enough to cross. John drove down winding roads to the lonely meeting place. He waited for hours as the family walked for miles toward him. It grew darker and more dangerous to travel.

When Carlos passed baby Anna to John, she screamed, grabbed his beard, and pulled hard. John was on the verge of screaming himself. Maria crossed next. Carlos and the other family crossed at another place for safety. With the tired mother and child, John drove back to town. He only saw car headlights, any of which could be border police.

Though frightened himself, John tried to talk to Maria, but she huddled with Anna. How frightened she must have been! Alone with a foreign man in the dark in a strange country! Only once the family reunited in town did Maria give John a shy smile.

On their long journey across the U.S., the refugees stayed with a different family each night. Each would call ahead to the next safe house and say, "The Lone Ranger is here." They gathered clothes and food, fueled the cars, and got ready to drive onward.

Meanwhile, the way opened! Both families came to our Sanctuary. Friends prepared space, scheduled helpers, and practiced Spanish. One morning, John and I woke at five and drove over the mountains to pick them up. We arrived as everyone was having breakfast. Before driving home, we sat on the back porch, drank coffee, and passed around those beautiful babies.

Now Anna is four. Both families brought our community so much joy! They cared for our children, taught us Guatemalan cooking, and shared their music and poetry. Our meeting held vigils, prayer services, and educational events about Central America. We had times of fear, misunderstanding, and hurt feelings. But over and over, we worked, listened, and struggled, and the way opened. We took the next step in our experiment with caring for each other in the Sanctuary Movement, protecting refugees fleeing violence in Central America or other places.

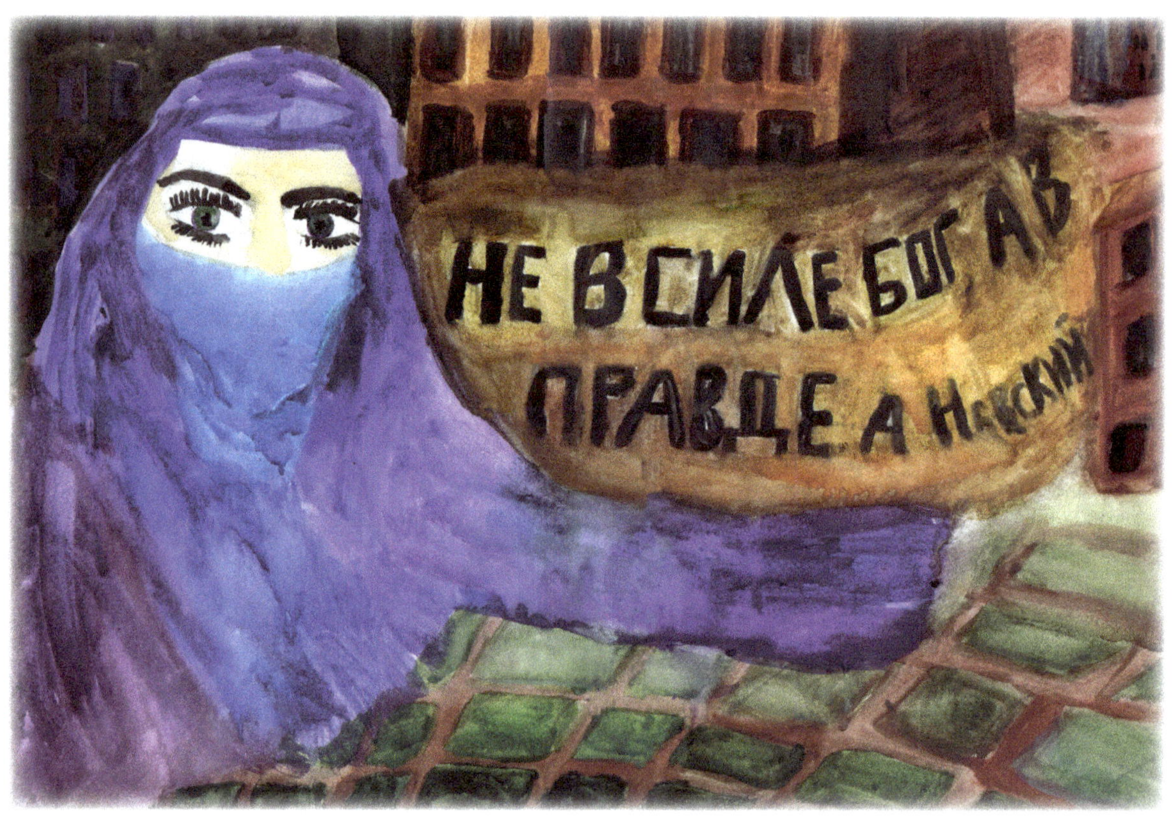

Nastasia Roshchina, age 17, 21 x 16.75 in. tempera

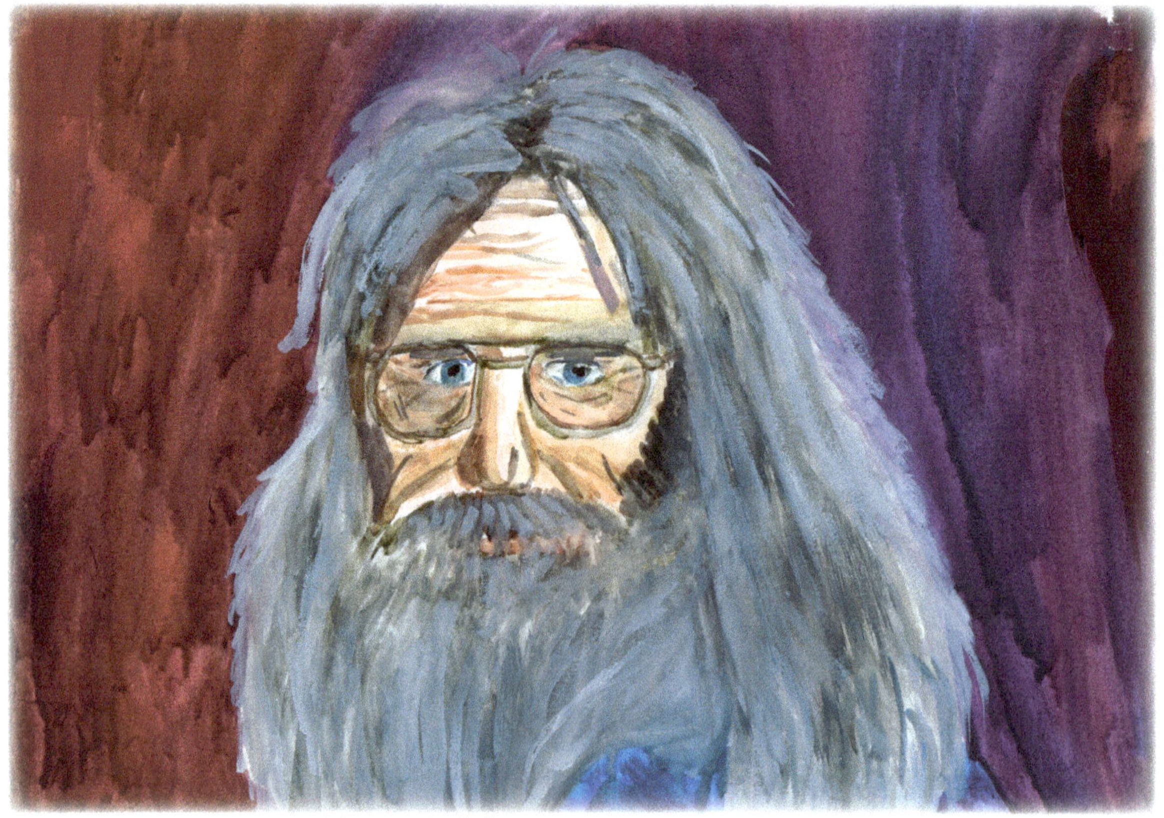

Nastasia Roshchina, age 17, 17 x 14 in. tempera

Vigil for Peace

by Mikhail Roshchin, Russia

The second Chechen War had raged for a month in October 1999. Refugees flooded out of Chechnya, while Moscow was peaceful. Few realized that a new tragedy would overwhelm an entire nation, and that the pathway of blood would not bring better understanding between Russians and Chechens.

I felt great concern and anxiety, because I could do nothing to stop these events. I called Viktor Popkov, an "Old Believer" of deep faith, who worked hard in Chechnya during the first war bringing humanitarian aid, arranging prisoner exchanges, and observing the short armistice in the summer of 1995.

We realized there would be no mass protests against this war. Most people felt sure the Chechens were to blame for the recent explosions in Moscow, and the press screamed, "Let our army finish the job!!"

Viktor proposed a hunger strike in solidarity with Chechnya's people. Words of the Russian Prince Alexander Nevsky were our motto: "Not by force! Oh God, but by truth." Our action began in Moscow beside the Solovetsky stone, site of a large camp for political prisoners in Stalinist times. We tied our banners to the stone as if it were our foundation stone. We took shelter behind it from the icy wind that shook our placards like sails.

We ate no food and drank only hot water. Near the stone, we made a small shelter of polythene plastic sheets. We placed devotional books and icons on a small table. We prayed for everyone who perished in the war, Chechens and Russians, Christians and Muslims.

We explained what we were doing, and why, to anyone who approached, and received support from many. I especially recall a woman who traveled from another town to meet us.

Nine days into our strike my friend, Moscow Quaker Sasha Gorbenko, replaced me. I asked him to fast for a week. He stayed on the hunger strike for 43 days until the Russian elections. He felt called to a significant commitment while blood was being shed and innocent people were dying. The strike's results were minimal, but we felt it better to act than to be silent while crime after crime was committed in the name of the Russian people.

After five weeks of his hunger strike, Viktor traveled to Chechnya to meet Chechen President, Aslan Maskhadov. He believed such a meeting could halt military activity. In December 1999, he flew to Sleptsovky in Ingushetia. The Chechens received this well-intentioned man of another faith with respect. He reached the villages of Urus-Martan and Valerik, but could not cross the front line into territory outside Federal forces' control.

In the winter of 2000, twice Viktor carried money into Chechnya and bought flour for the villagers. In the Spring he met with President Maskhadov, but the road to peace proved harder than expected. The war sowed new seeds of hatred every day.

But I still believe that only by tearing hatred from our hearts can we set out to meet each other and learn that nothing is more precious than peace.

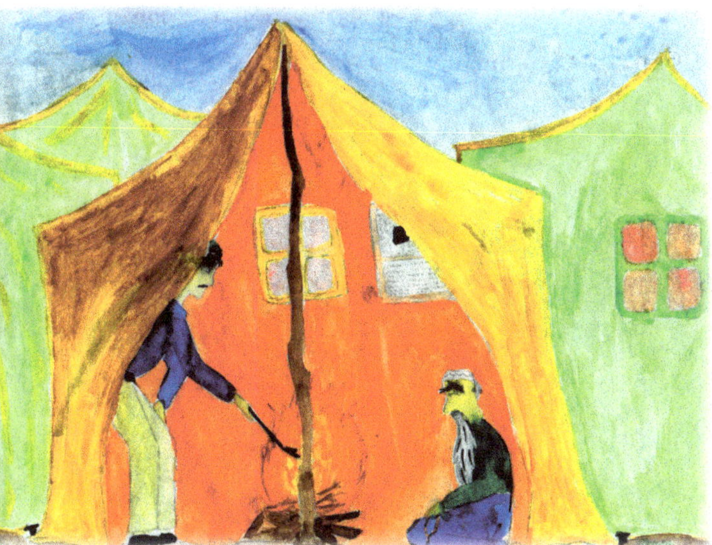

Diana Mamieva, age 15, 11.75 x 8 in. watercolor

Part 4: Love and Hope

Stories from Chechnya, France, Germany, Ukraine, the UK, and the USA

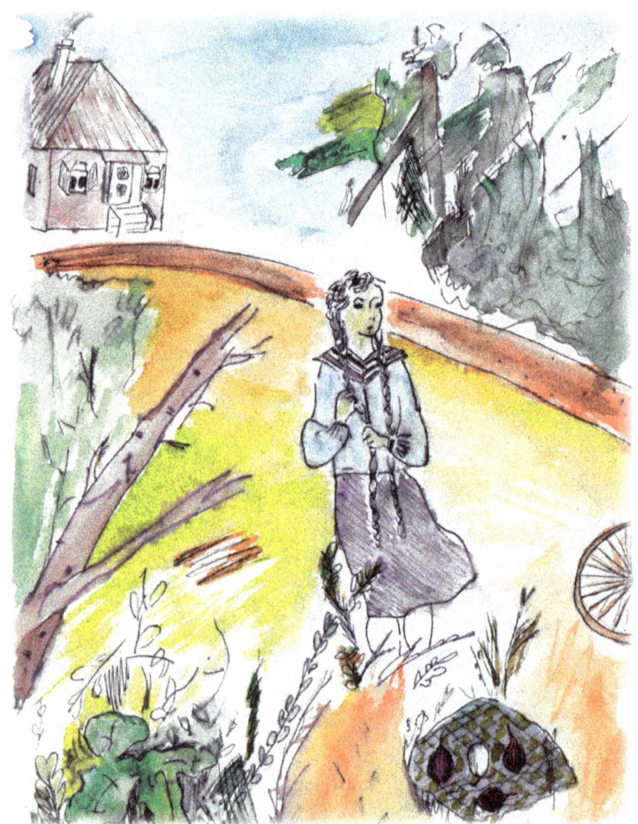

Ulya Badayeva, age unknown, 7 x 10.5 in. ink & watercolor

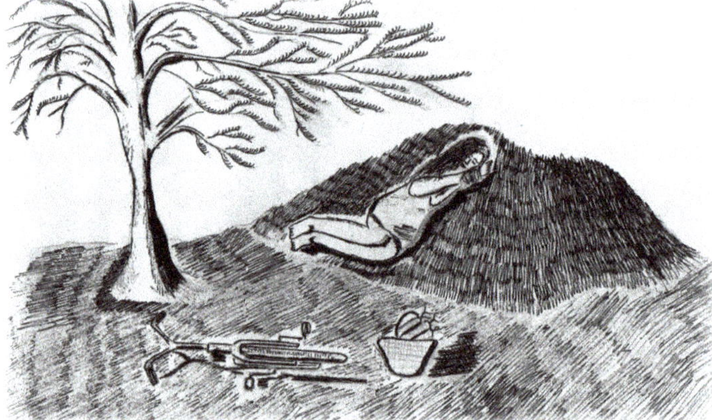

Anzor Elmurzayev, 11 x 7 in. ink and pencil

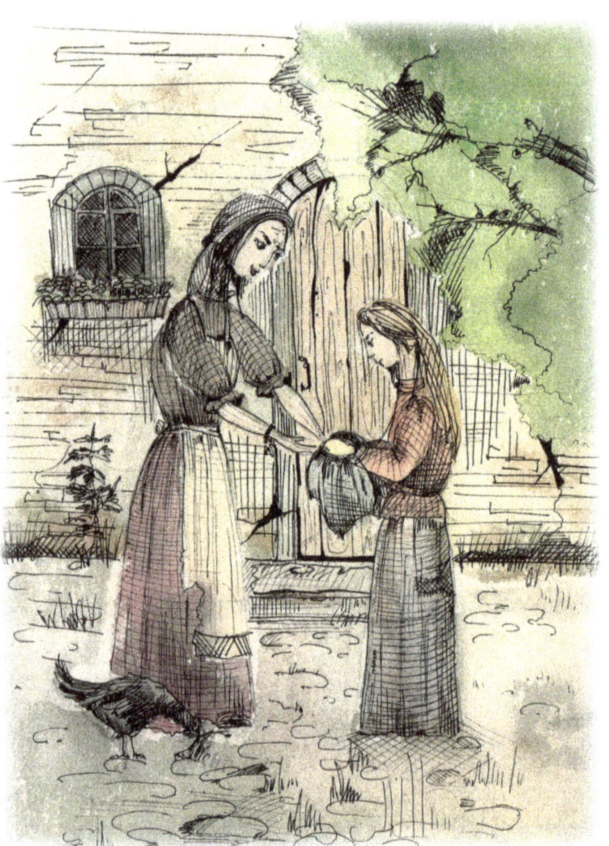

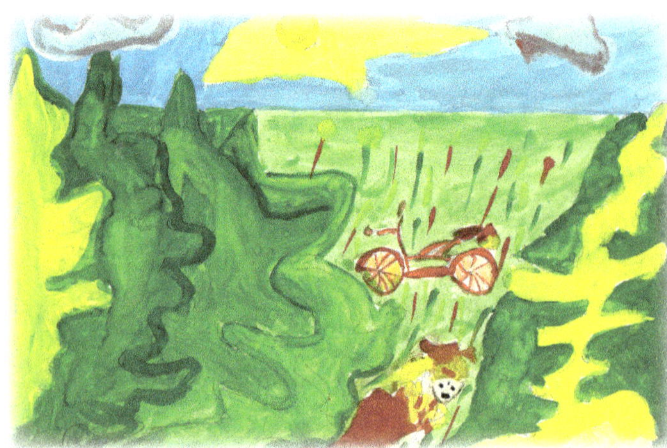

Zaira Kurbanova, age 11, 11.5 x 8 in. watercolor

Nastasya Gagarinskaya, age 14 8.25x11 in. ink watercolor

Anna and the Speckled Hen

by Ruth Hunt Gefvert, Germany

Food was scarce in Germany during World War II. People were hungry, especially children. Anna looked for food on her weekly bicycle ride to the country. She was so tired she pushed the bike slowly. Even that made her heart race. She was tired all the time these days, and discouraged. Except for a few beets, no one had any food to give or sell.

Suddenly she could go no further. She lay down in the cool grass beside her bicycle and dreamed of golden carrots, steaming hot in cream and butter. Even in her dream she knew this was foolish. She had never tasted butter or cream, but her mother had described them. She dreamed of tomatoes too, beautiful red, juicy ones. Anna was about to eat one when they disappeared. She woke with a start, rolled over, and there, looking her right in the eye, was a speckled hen. They looked at each other–Anna and the speckled hen.

"Why are you staring at me, you silly thing?" asked Anna. "And waking me up!"

"Cu-u-u-t . . ." said the hen, backing away.

Then Anna saw the egg! Carefully, she picked it up, still warm. "Oh, you beautiful, beautiful hen!" she exclaimed. "I'm sorry I was rude. Thank you for this lovely egg!"

Anna felt better now. She took her scarf off and carefully wrapped the egg. She got on her bicycle to hurry home to her mother. But then a terrible thought crossed her mind: the egg wasn't hers. It belonged to the owner of the speckled hen. Anna pedaled slower. "No! The egg is mine. The hen laid it right beside me." Anna pedaled on. But as she approached a little white house close to the road, her legs wouldn't pedal. Very slowly, she got off her bicycle and walked to the house.

"Yes?" asked the young woman at the door.

Reluctantly, with her dream of a small omelet fading, Anna said, "Do… do… you own a… a…. speckled hen?"

"Why yes!" exclaimed the woman.

Carefully, Anna unwrapped her scarf and handed the egg to the woman. "Then this is yours," she said in a small voice.

"Oh, thank you," said the woman. "That hen lays eggs everywhere. We need her eggs for our little boy. He's very sick. You're so kind," she said. "I wish I had something to give you, but there is so little. I… I… have nothing to give you."

"It's all right," said Anna as she climbed onto her bicycle, anxious to get away from the little white house, the speckled hen, and the wonderful egg.

At home Anna told her mother, afraid her mother would scold her for being late, for bringing only a few beets, or for not keeping the egg. But her mother only smoothed Anna's hair with a smile.

"Then you're not angry with me, Mother? You don't think I'm too young to go to the country to bargain for vegetables?"

"No, Anna," said her mother. "I'm just thinking what a fine daughter I have. When one is so hungry all the time, only a very wise person could have made such a hard decision to return the egg."

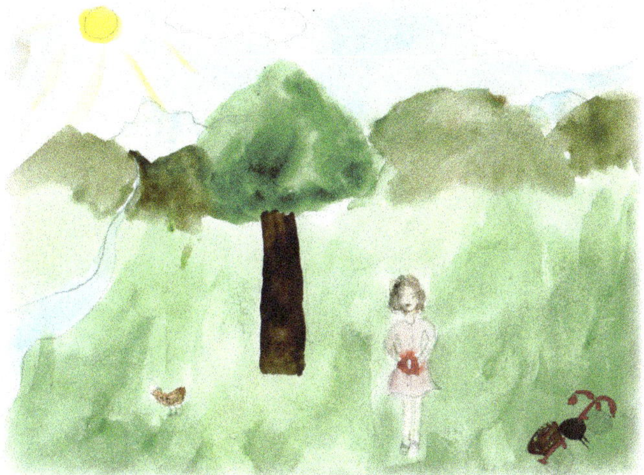

Emap Mamayeva, age 11, 11 x 8.25 in. watercolor

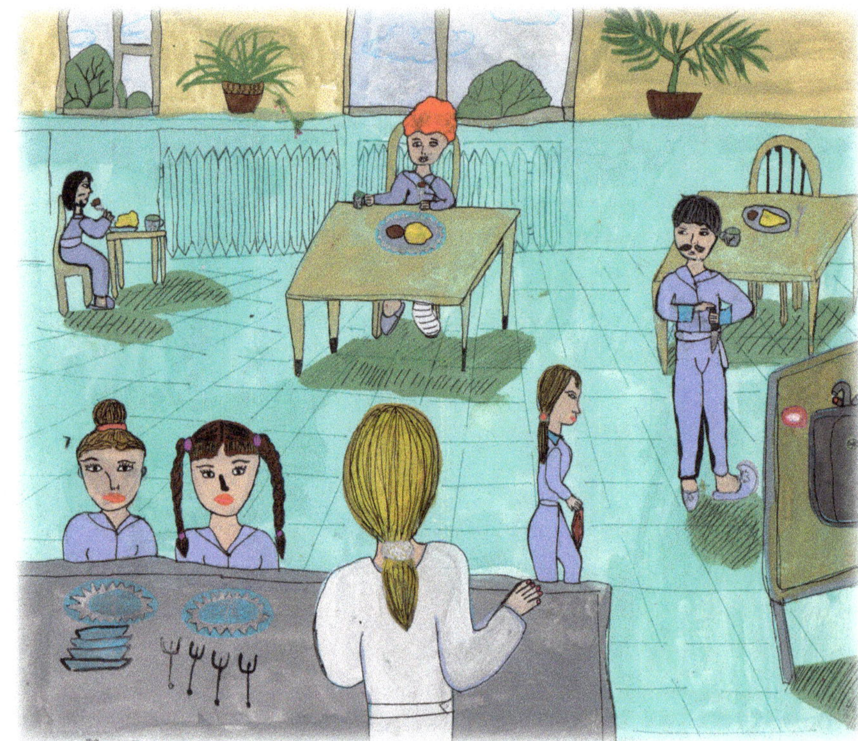

Alyona Kusmina
age 10
16.5 x 11.75 in.
tempera

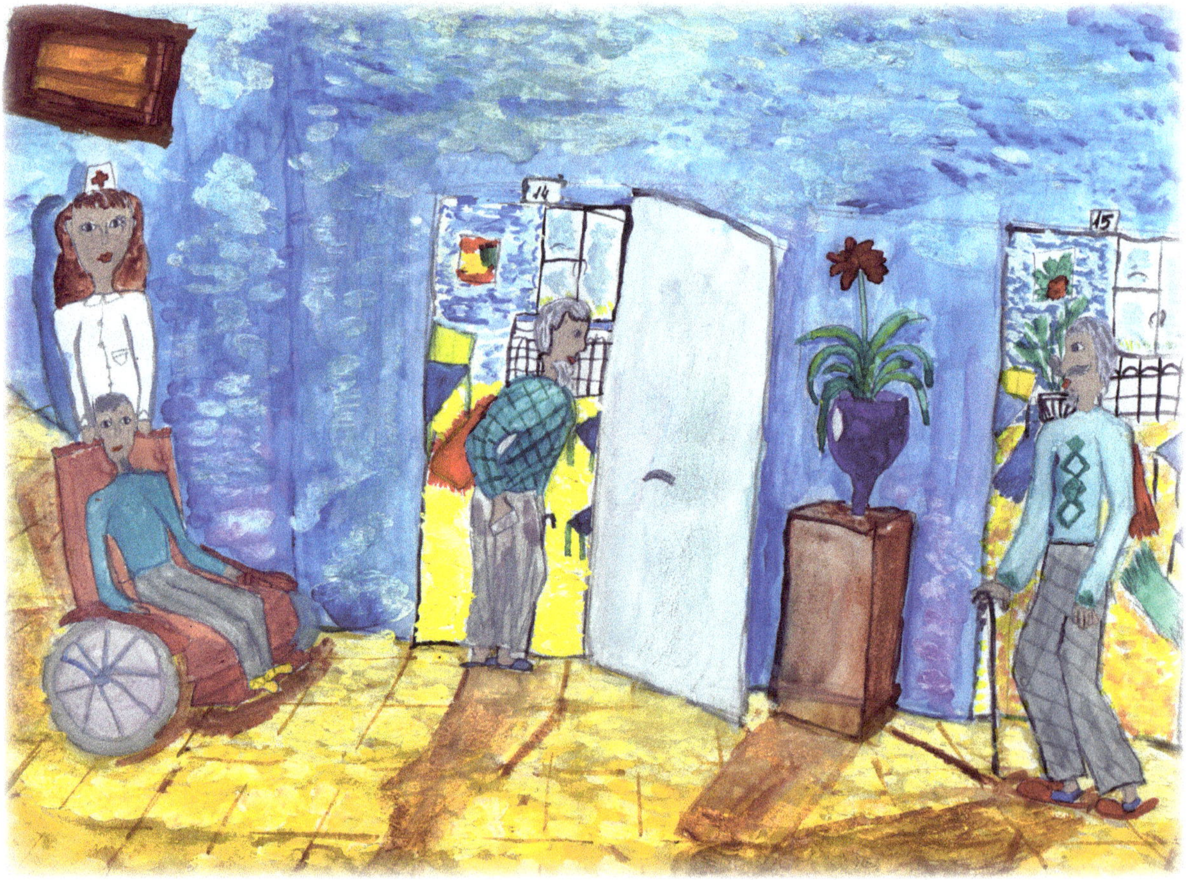

Katia Baikina, age 9, 17 x 12 in. tempera

$\mathscr{Bocha}$

by Musa Akhmadov, Chechnya

Bocha was over 70 years old, and a hospital patient for the first time in his life. For a while, he considered just going to join his father, who had died in a forced labor camp years ago, but a dream of his father convinced Bocha to let the doctor perform the kidney operation he needed.

The operation was successful, and Dr. Khaid was so kind and caring that Bocha was determined to find a special gift to thank him for saving his life. No gift seemed quite right, so when Bocha heard that Dr. Khaid's own father was a patient in the hospital, he was determined to visit him, chat with him, and show him some of the kindness that his son, the doctor, had shown Bocha.

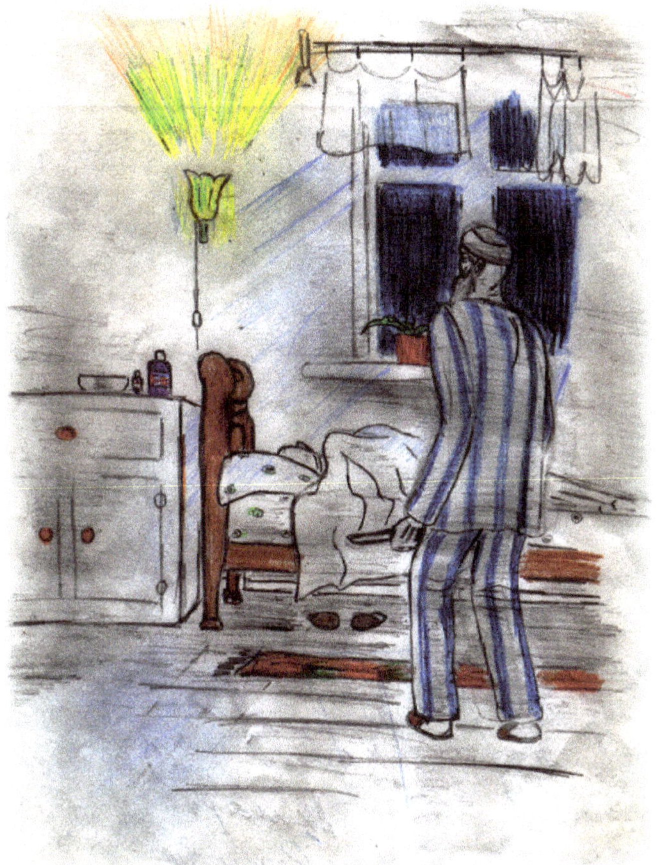

Unknown, 8.75 x 11.5 in. pencil and colored pencil

Imagine his surprise, then, when he found Dr. Khaid's father, and recognized him as a man he'd searched for all his life – Barznak, the man whose false testimony had sent not only Bocha's father, but his two brothers as well, to the labor camp to die all those years ago! Bocha had sworn revenge then – and here was his chance. But this man's son had saved Bocha's life. How could Bocha kill his father? How could he face his father if he let this man go free? These voices argued back and forth in his heart all day.

In the evening, he took a bread-knife from the dining hall and crept into the father's ward. As Barznak slept fitfully, Bocha found many excuses to put off the moment of revenge. Finally, however, he forced his legs to move. He pushed open the door into the ward, then he stopped. He stood still with his back against the wall and realized that he would never be able to carry out the plan. Just when he drew the knife and started to go into the ward, a vision of the good doctor appeared to him, stopping him, forcing him to back off.

"How do you feel?" the good doctor in the white coat sitting by his bedside was asking him. "Everything's fine. You'll soon be on your feet. You'll have to put off dying till another day. Now then, let's check your pulse." He felt the touch of Khaid's sensitive fingers on his arm.

This whole vision took place in a single second. The knife made a noise when he threw it on the floor, but nobody woke up. Tears ran down Bocha's cheeks. He felt angry and helpless. He wanted to howl at the top of his voice throughout the sleeping hospital. The feeling of revenge that had driven him for decades was overcome by the power of compassion.

He could never lift a hand against the man who had saved his life. This new understanding was to be his gift to Dr. Khaid.

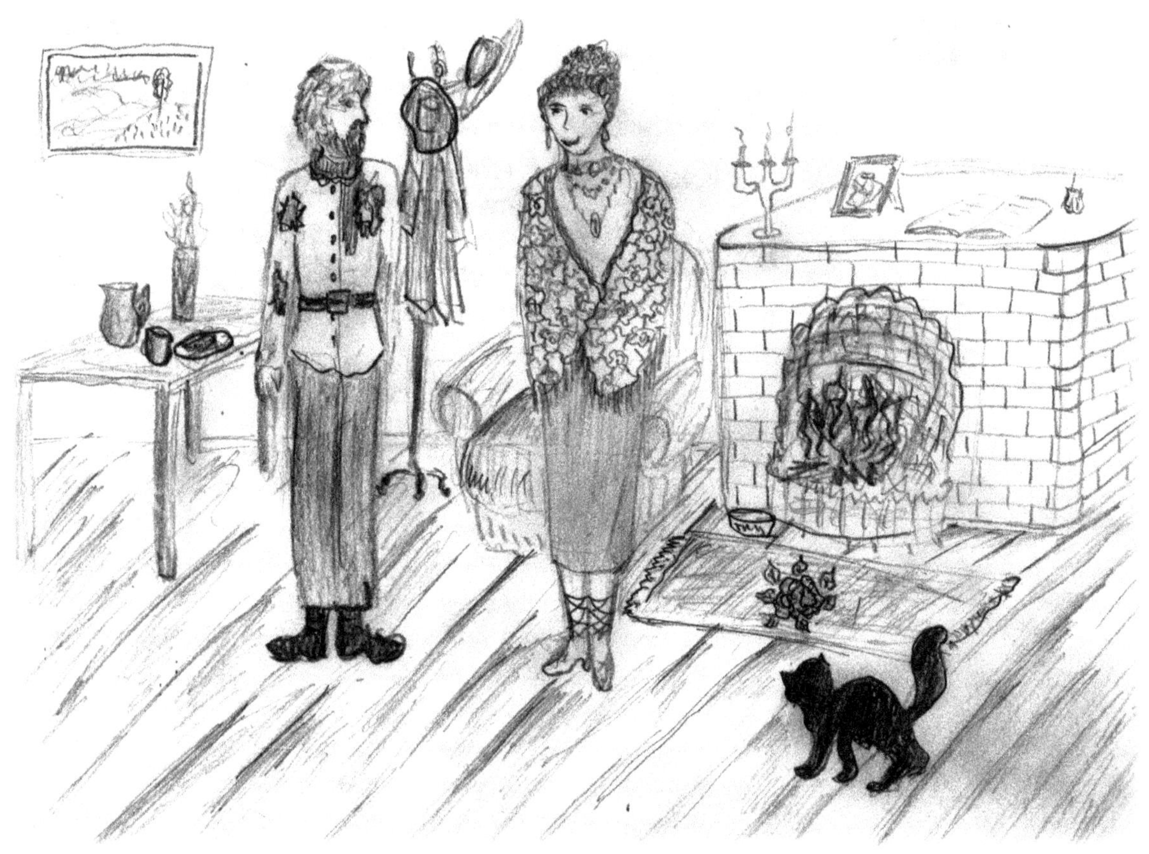

Alicia Reichman, age 10, 8.25 x 6.75 in. pencil

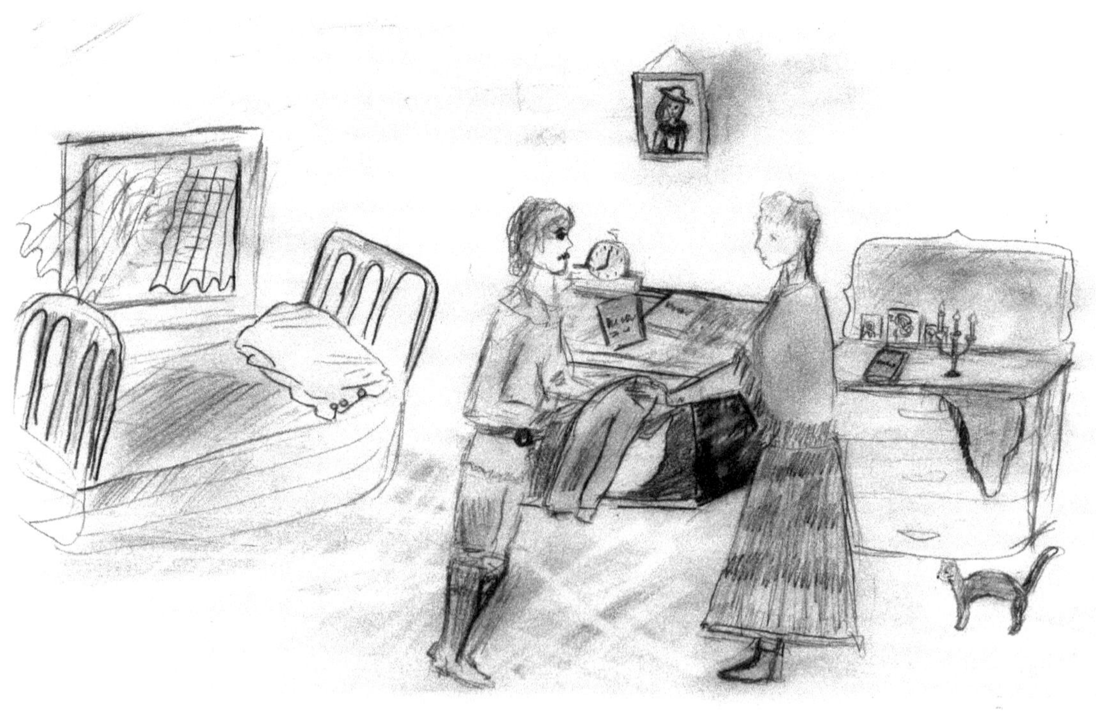

Alicia Reichman, age 10, 11.74 x 8.25 in. pencil

Boot under the Bed

by Murry Engle Lauser, United Kingdom

In spite of her heavy wool skirt and shawl, Elizabeth Fry was chilled from her day in the drafty Bristol women's prison. "It's not fit for anyone, no matter what their crime! But those poor children! What could I do to help occupy their minds and hands?" Elizabeth thought as she climbed the winding stairs in the old stone inn.

When she opened the door to her room, she sensed something strange. A dresser drawer was ajar, and a candle tipped over. Just visible under the bed was a man's boot.

She gasped. What should she do? As she quietly closed the drawer and picked up the candle, she reached a decision. She knelt beside the boot, hearing someone breathing under the bed. "Dear God," she began, "please forgive this man. May thy goodness enter his heart and help him to improve his ways." Her voice was so kind. The boot stirred. "This man is confused and needs thy guidance to stop stealing."

The man crawled out from under the bed. He was thin and unshaven. "Why are you praying for me?" he asked gruffly. "Why don't you call the innkeeper and get it over with?"

"God is the only one I'll call," said Elizabeth. She was still afraid but looked at him kindly, "Thee must have a reason to come to my room." His shoulders drooped. "Can't thee tell me?" she asked. The man remained silent. Elizabeth waited.

"I've been hungry for days, Ma'am," he said at last. "I stole scraps of food, but it's not enough. I need money for a good meal and a warm coat too."

"I'm glad thee came to my room," said Elizabeth.

The man looked at her in amazement. He had never been treated so kindly, even when he worked as a stagecoach footman. Elizabeth pulled a heavy sweater from the drawer. "This was my husband's," she said. "I think it will fit thee. Now let's go downstairs for dinner."

"You're sure good to me," he said. "You could have sent me to prison—or will you?" His eyes darted wildly toward the window.

"No," she said. "I know too much about prisons to send anyone there." Seeing his puzzlement, she added, "I'll tell thee at dinner."

While they ate boiled mutton and potatoes, she told him about her prison work and he told her about his troubles. First he had gone to prison for an unpaid debt, then for stealing, and then for a false accusation. Since his release, he could not get a job. His clothes were worn and dirty, so no one trusted him. He wanted to stay out of prison so much he almost starved before coming to her room. Elizabeth had heard similar stories from women in prison.

In her practical way, Elizabeth gave the man soap, clean clothes, and help in finding a job. He left with strength in his body and hope in his heart. Elizabeth felt a deep sense of peace, grateful she had responded with love rather than fear.

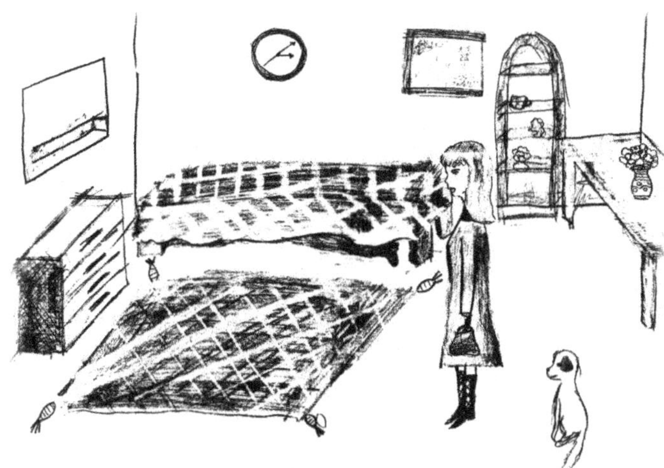

Alicia Reichman, age 10, 11.75 x 8.25 in. pencil

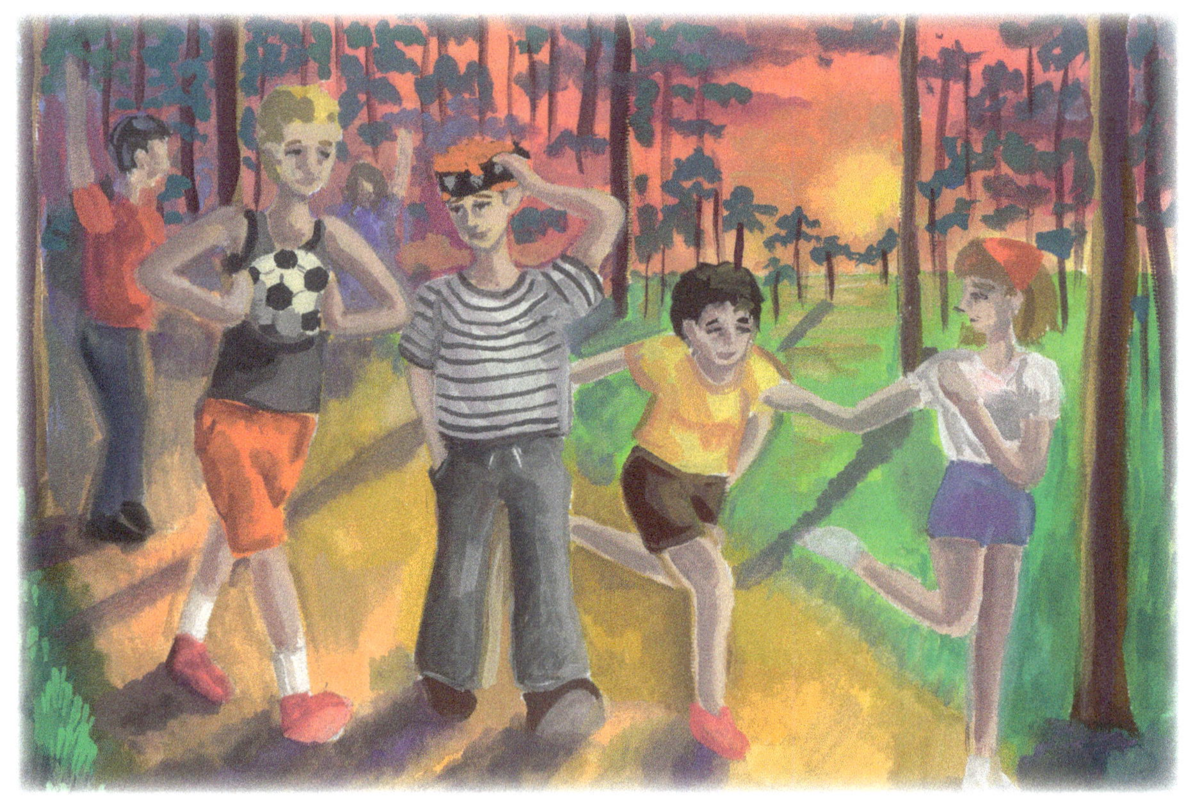

Gorbatova Kateryna, age 16, tempera

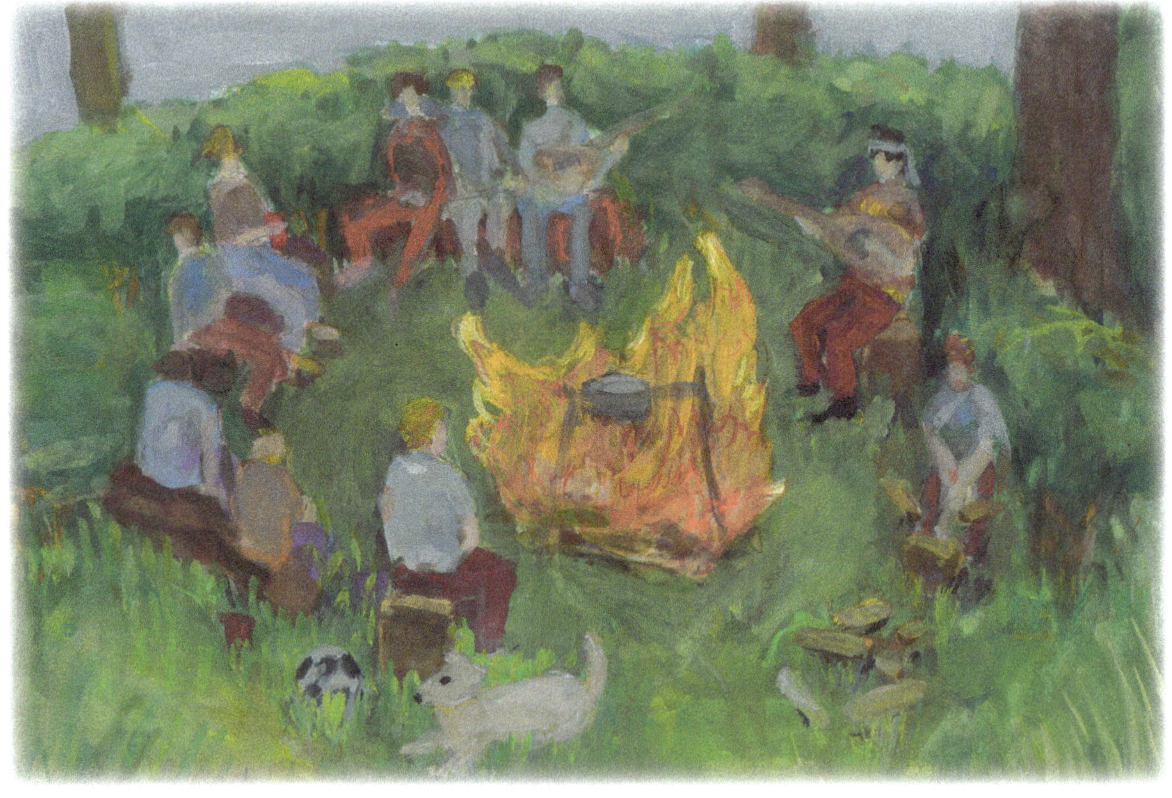

Kycheryavaya Maria, age 16, tempera

Camping for Peace

by Inga Danilchenko, Ukraine

The first day of summer camp in Rovno was quite an adventure for the kids on Team 7. They came from broken homes in remote villages in the northern Chernobyl districts in northern Ukraine. They wore cheap clothes and spoke in an odd dialect of mixed Ukrainian, Russian, and Belorussian. For many it was their first trip outside their home village.

A smiling boy named Sashko was always encouraging and reassuring his friends. Short and stocky, dressed in short, baggy pants, a faded t-shirt, and a pair of old canvas sneakers, Sashko soon became the uncontested leader of Team 7.

Despite their fears, they survived their first day at camp. On the second day, Team 2 showed up, a group of tough hipsters wearing baseball caps, rapper-style bright t-shirts, and fancy sneakers. Their leader, called Dimych, wore a flashy bandana.

Around adults Dimych behaved as a polite, mature, and responsible young man. But out of their sight, he had clearly picked Sashko as his main target, and set out to get him in any way he could. He walked straight into Sashko, pretending not to see him, then mimicked Sashko's rural dialect and laughed. He insulted Sashko by asking loudly, "Have you figured out you need to wash up before you come to eat?" Decked out in his most stylish clothes, Dimych pointed out Sashko's shabby clothes at the dance party, saying loudly, "You can bet his whole village chipped in to buy those shoes."

Dimych's teammates picked on others from Sashko's team, and rumors began to spread of an impending brawl. Suddenly, a special event was announced. Two teams at a time would go on a camping trip together away from the main camp. The first would be Teams 2 and 7! How well they organized and cooperated would determine how often others got to go camping.

The whole camp was excited, and the boys on Teams 2 and 7 were determined to make a good showing. One of their first tasks was to build a fire.

Those who had never held an axe in their life had to be quick learners.

"Keep your hatchet slightly at an angle. It's easier that way," Tolik from Team 7 explained.

Then it was time to cook. Pascha, from town, took the lead. His father was a chef in one of the best restaurants. He taught everyone something, from slicing vegetables to using onions in new ways. When it was time to eat, it was the village boys who improvised a table out of tent stakes and a board.

On breaks, two town boys performed masterfully on guitars, followed by the village boys singing Cossack songs in harmony. Enthusiasm for all the music ran high.

Then came a soccer game. Teams 2 and 7 were mixed. Dimych and Sashko ended up on the same team. As Dimych played striker and Sashko played goalie, the crowd cheered for both players. When the match was over, all the heroes were picked up and carried around. As the tired boys wandered back towards camp, Dimych's bandana was clearly visible on Sasko's head. Once rivals, they had truly become very dirty, but very happy friends.

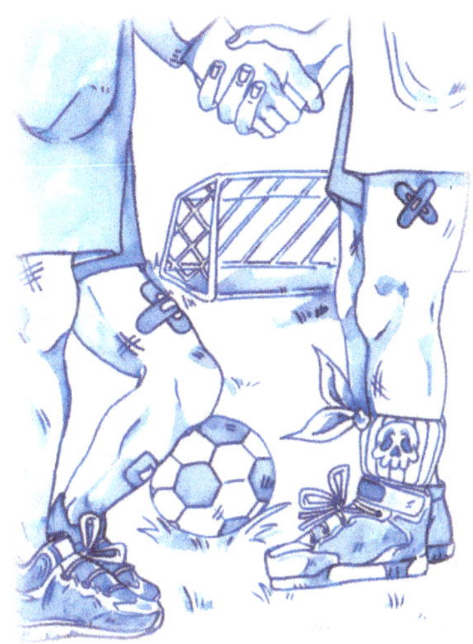

Kireeva Vlada, age 18, ink and watercolor

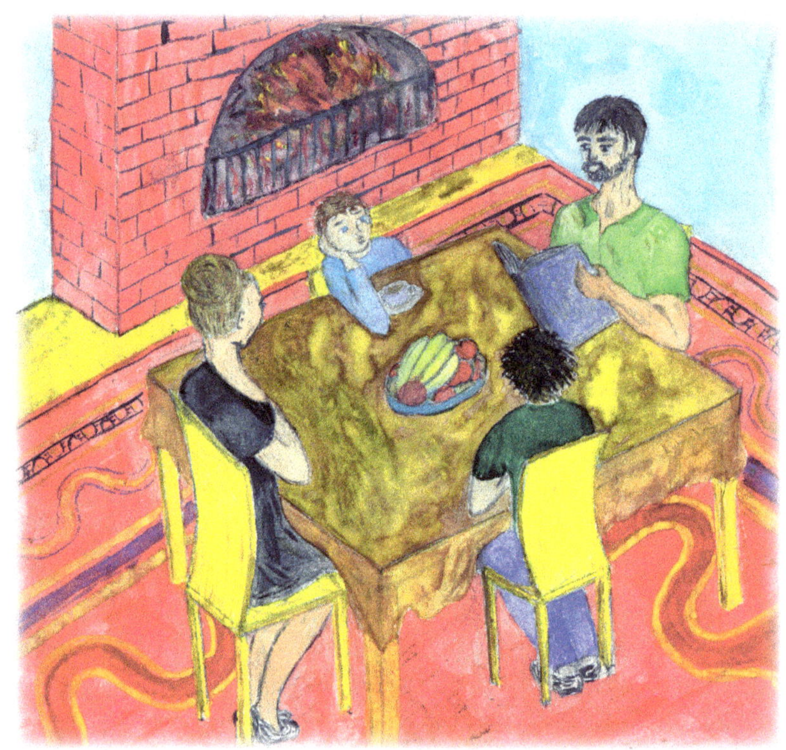

Anzor Hashagulov, 8.25 x 8 in. watercolor

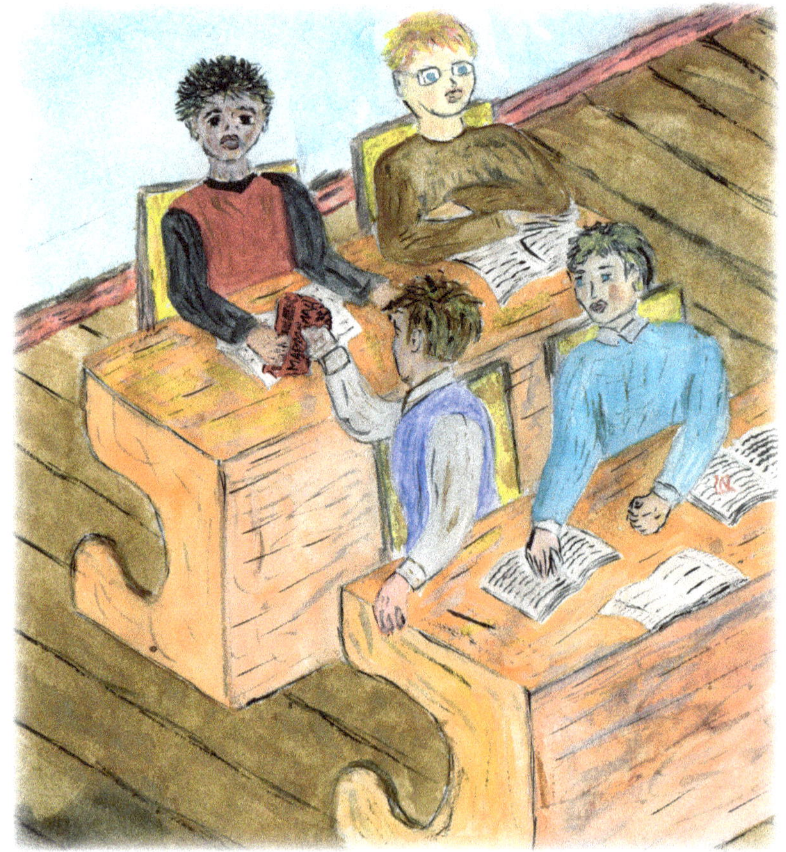

Anzor Hashagulov, 5.75 x 6.75 in. watercolor

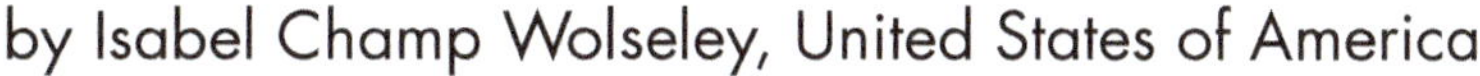
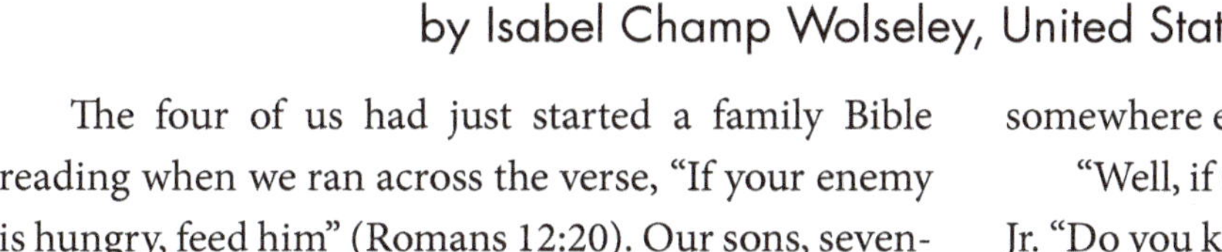

Jelly Beans

by Isabel Champ Wolseley, United States of America

The four of us had just started a family Bible reading when we ran across the verse, "If your enemy is hungry, feed him" (Romans 12:20). Our sons, seven- and ten-years-old, were especially puzzled. "Why should you feed your enemy?" they wondered.

My husband and I wondered too. John's only answer was, "We're supposed to because God says so." We never thought we would soon learn this from experience.

Day after day, John Jr. came home from school complaining about a classmate who sat behind him in fifth grade. "Bob keeps jabbing me when Miss Smith isn't looking. One of these days when we're on the playground, I'm going to jab him right back!"

I was ready to go to the school and jab Bob myself. Obviously the boy was a brat. Besides, why wasn't Miss Smith doing a better job? I'd better give her a verbal jab, too. I was still stewing over this injustice to John Jr. when his younger brother startled all of us by saying, "Maybe he should feed his enemy."

None of us was sure about this "enemy" business. It didn't seem that an enemy would be in fifth grade. An enemy was someone who was way off, well, somewhere else not here.

"Well, if God says so you'd better do it," I told John Jr. "Do you know what Bob likes to eat? If you're going to feed him, you may as well get something he likes."

Our elder son thought for a moment. "Jelly beans!" he shouted. "Bob loves jelly beans." So we bought a bag of jellybeans for our son to take to school the next day. We would see whether enemy-feeding worked.

That night we discussed the strategy to use. The next time Bob jabbed him, John Jr. would turn around and put a bag of jellybeans on his desk.

The next afternoon I waited patiently for the school bus to pull up, then dashed out to meet the boys. John Jr. called ahead, "It worked, Mom! It worked!"

His little brother claimed responsibility for the success. "Hey, remember, it was my idea."

I wanted details, "What did Bob do? What did he say?"

"He was so surprised he didn't say anything—he just took the jellybeans. But he didn't jab me the rest of the day!" It wasn't long before John Jr. and Bob became friends—all because of a little bag of jellybeans.

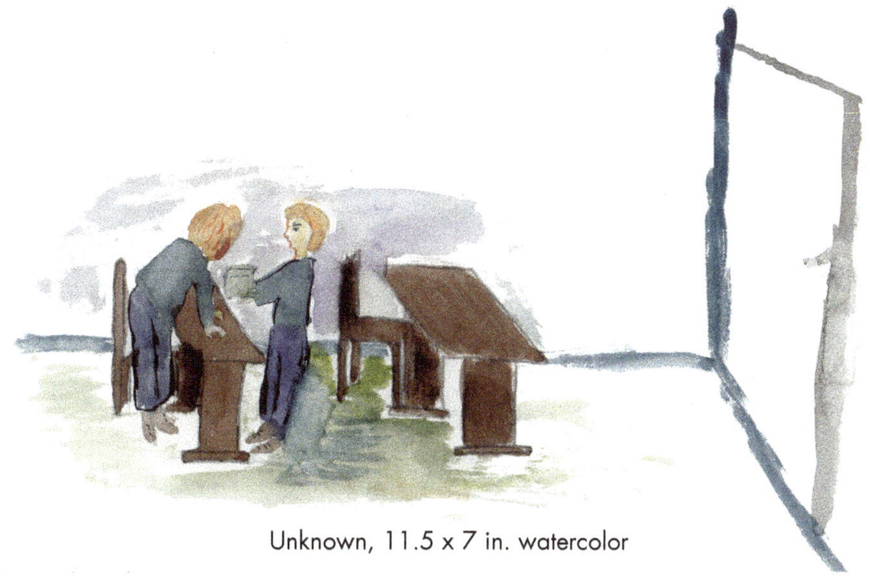

Unknown, 11.5 x 7 in. watercolor

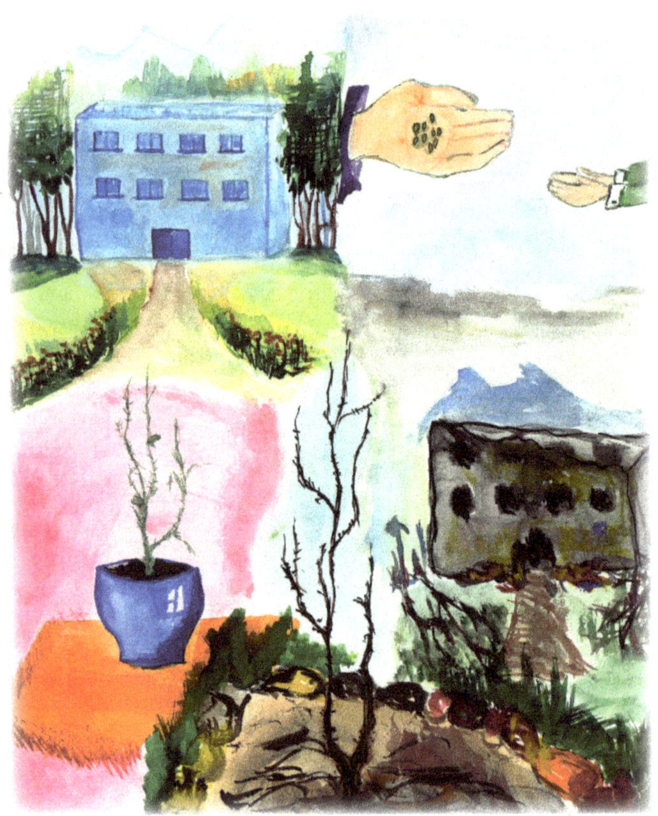

Zarema Halustova, 10 x 14.5 in. watercolor

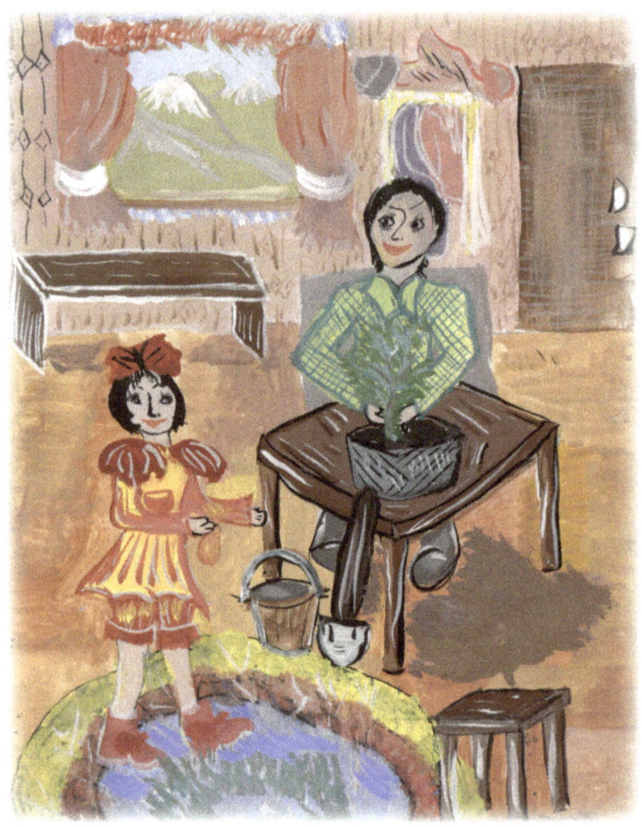

Ania Hopta, age 8 16.25 in. x 11 in. tempera

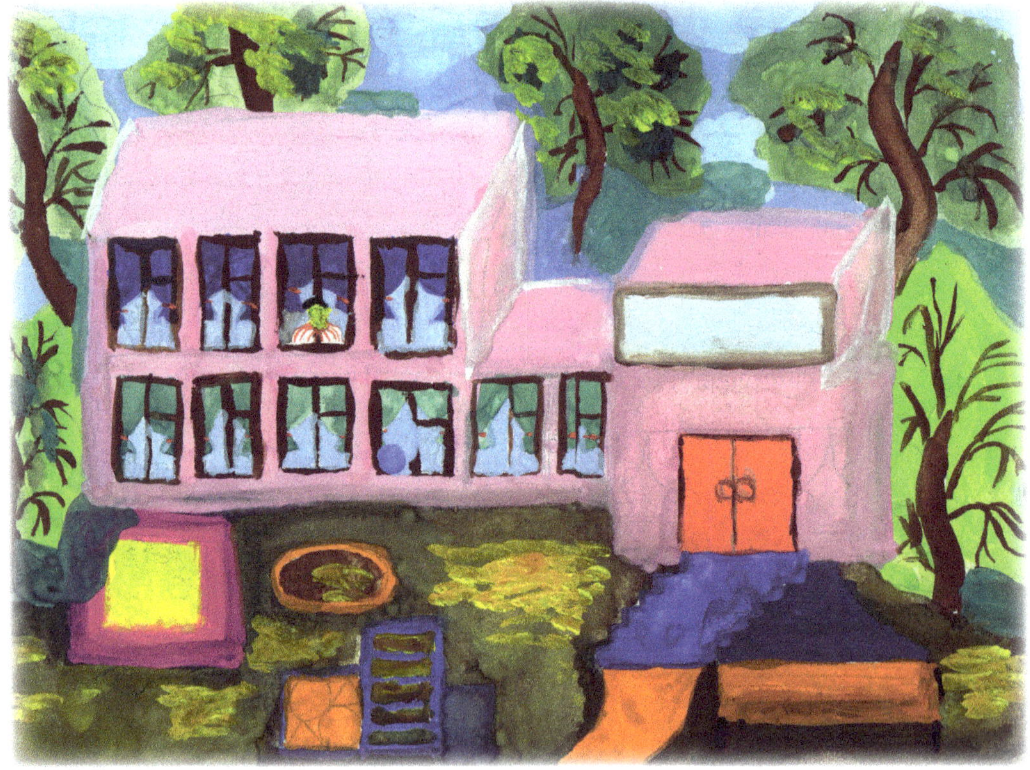

Natasha Ulasevich, age 8, 14.5 x 9.5 in. tempera

Seeds of Hope

by Victor Lozinsky with Deborah J. Rasmussen, Chechnya/Russia

I lived in a building in Chechnya that had once been a kindergarten, near the village of Samashki in the resort area of Sernovodsk. The yard around my building was full of tall, thorny acacia trees. These trees hid much of the outside world from view. Sometimes I could almost imagine that Sernovodsk was still a resort.

But the trees could not hide the truth. The sound of cannon fire and bombers overhead brought reality all too close. In April of 1995 Chechnya and Russia were at war. Sernovodsk was now a refugee camp. I was part of a group of international human rights observers. The situation seemed more and more impossible, even hopeless. What would come of all this killing and destruction?

When I went home, I took with me some of the longest seedpods from the acacia trees and a branch covered with enormous thorns. I knew that my small son Kirill would find them interesting. Sure enough, he planted several seeds in a flowerpot.

Before long, more sad news came from Chechnya. Samashki was attacked again and Sernovodsk had fallen. The former kindergarten no longer existed. And all of those rugged acacias, I learned, were gone.

Not quite all.

A single fragile sprout peeped through the soil in the heart of Russia. We cared for it, watered it, watched it gradually uncurl into a sturdy plant and reach toward the light. When it was ready, we planted it outside, hoping it would continue to grow.

Years have passed since then. In many countries, disagreements still turn into war. Somewhere amid the blood and death, fragile life still breaks through when we plant the seeds of peace and tend the soil. All is not lost. At my home, in Russia, a Chechen acacia tree grows.

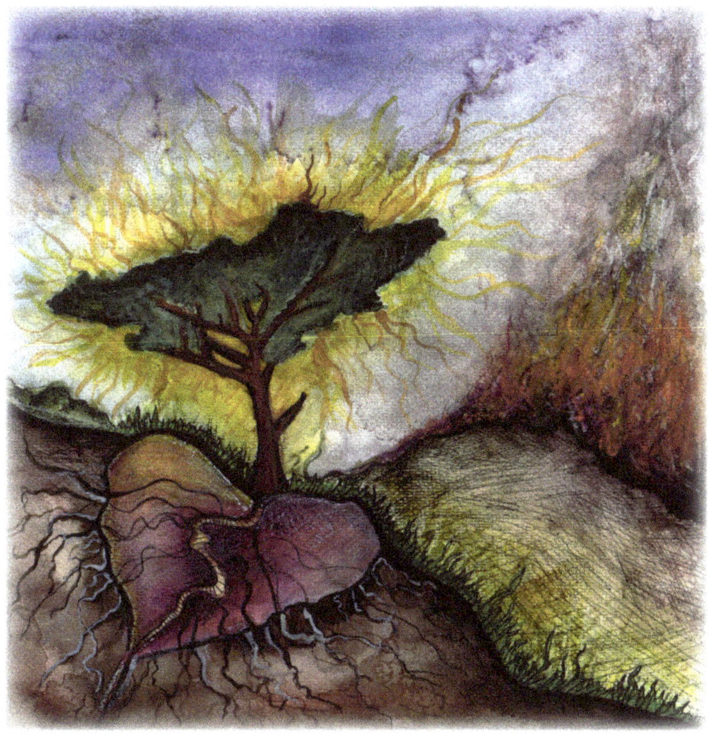

Hilary Amborn, 9.75 x 10.25 in. watercolor on canvas

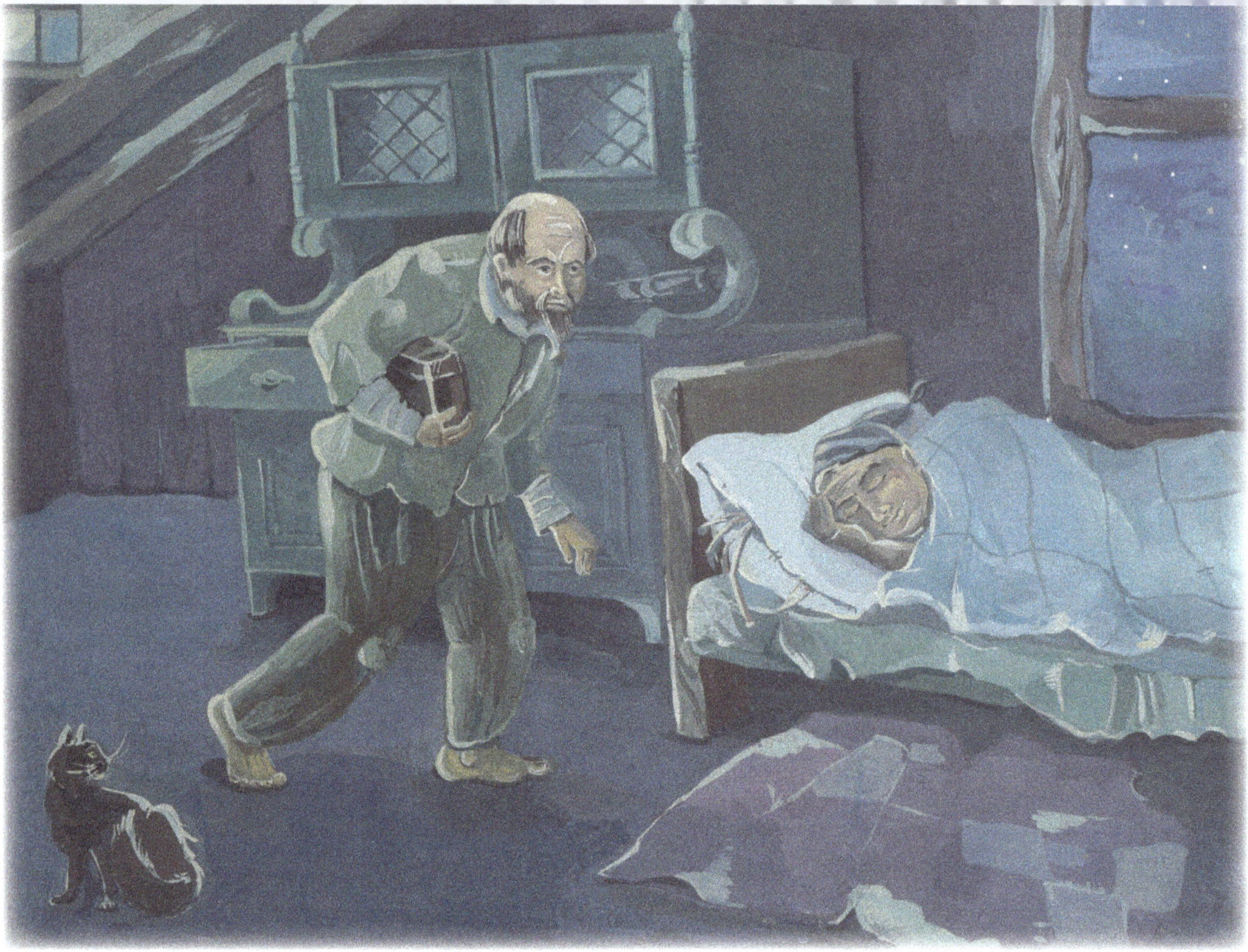

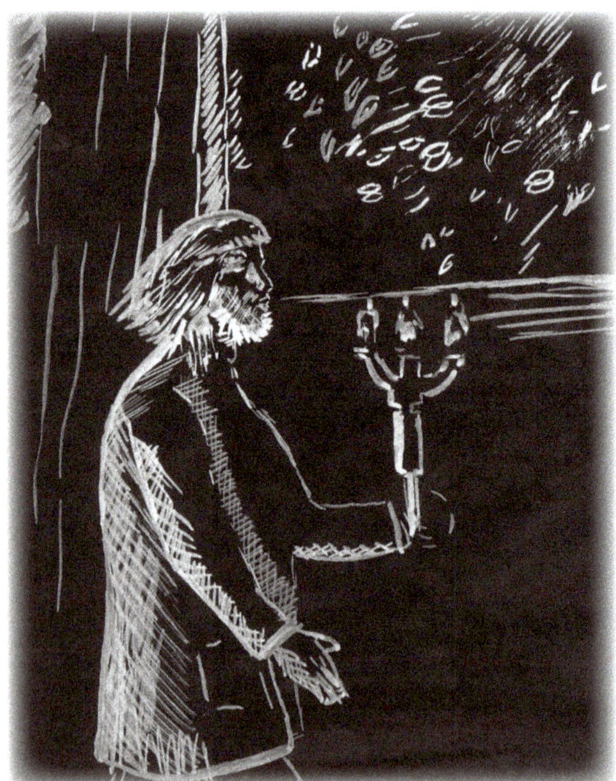

Natasha Ulasevich, age 8, 14.5 x 9.5 in. tempera

"We share a faith

– across religion, class and culture- -

in the power of the Living Spirit to give life,

joy, peace, and prosperity through love,

integrity, and compassionate justice among

people who live in simplicity, equality, and

nonviolence."

~ New York Yearly Meeting of the
Religious Society of Friends (Quakers), 2007

Saiyeva Malika, age 19, 8.75 x 11.25 in.
etching in black paint

Silver Candlesticks

adapted by Mikhail Roshchin and John Coutts from *Les Miserables* by Victor Hugo, France

In 1855, Charles François Bienvenu Myriel had freely chosen a simple life as Bishop of Digne for nearly 50 years. He gave to the needy, sick, and suffering. If anyone was in need, people would point the way to the Bishop's house.

In October, an hour before sunset, a traveller entered Digne on foot. Nobody let him in their house, but an old lady pointed to the Bishop's door. He rapped on the door, and the Bishop replied, "Come in." The man said loudly, "My name is Jean Valjean. I've done 19 years as a convict. They let me out four days ago. I'm very tired and terribly hungry."

The Bishop said to the housekeeper, "Please set another place and kindly put clean sheets on a bed." Then the Bishop turned to the man. "Sit down and warm yourself, sir. It's nearly time for supper. Your bed will be prepared while we eat."

Every time he said sir, the man's face lit up. To say sir to a convict is like giving a glass of water to a man dying of thirst.

"Father," said the traveler, "you are truly kind. You don't despise me. You accept me as a friend and light your fine candles for me, even though I've told you where I've come from, and what a poor devil I am." The Bishop said, "Only one person is at home here: the one who needs shelter."

When dinner was over, the Bishop picked up one of the silver candlesticks and gave the other to his guest. "Let me lead you to your room, sir," he said. The man followed him.

"I hope you sleep well," said the Bishop.

"Thank you, Father," he said.

Jean Valjean woke just as the cathedral clock struck two in the morning. He had noticed the silver forks and spoons and great ladle, and taken careful note of the cupboard in the Bishop's bedroom where the housekeeper had put them away. He held his breath and walked soundlessly towards the room where the bishop was sleeping.

Jean Valjean walked quickly along the bed. He opened the cupboard and seized the basket with all the silver. He thrust the silver into his knapsack, leapt into the garden, threw away the basket and bounded over the wall like a tiger.

Next morning, the housekeeper came running in a state of panic. "Sir! Sir!" she shouted. "Does Your Eminence know where the basket of silver is?" "Yes," said the Bishop. He had just picked up the basket in a flower bed and handed it to her. "But there's nothing in it," she said. "Where's the silver?"

"Ah," said the Bishop, "I have no idea where it is."

"Good Lord. It's been stolen …by that man who came here last night!"

The Bishop stood silent for a moment, then looked earnestly up at her and said gently, "By the way, did that silver really belong to us?" A few minutes later, as they were finishing breakfast, there came a knock at the door. The door opened and three policemen holding Jean Valjean by the collar appeared on the threshold. One walked up to the Bishop. "My Lord Bishop," he said.

Jean Valjean looked crushed. "My Lord Bishop?" he muttered. "So he isn't just the local priest?"

"Be quiet!" said one of the policemen, "This gentleman is indeed My Lord Bishop."

Meanwhile, the Bishop came forward. "Ah! There you are!" he said, looking at Jean Valjean. "I'm glad to see you. I gave you the candlesticks as well." Jean Valjean gave the Bishop a look that no language could describe.

"So," said the Corporal, "is what this man told us true?"

The Bishop smiled, "He told you that it had been given to him by an old priest who had given him a bed for the night." Jean Valjean staggered backward as the policemen let him go. "My friend," the Bishop went on, "before you go, you must take your candlesticks." He went to the mantel to fetch the two candlesticks, which he gave to Jean Valjean. "Now go in peace," said the Bishop. Then he turned to the policemen and said, "Gentlemen, you may leave us." They did so.

The Bishop said quietly to Jean Valjean, "Never forget that you promise me to use this money in order to become an honest man."

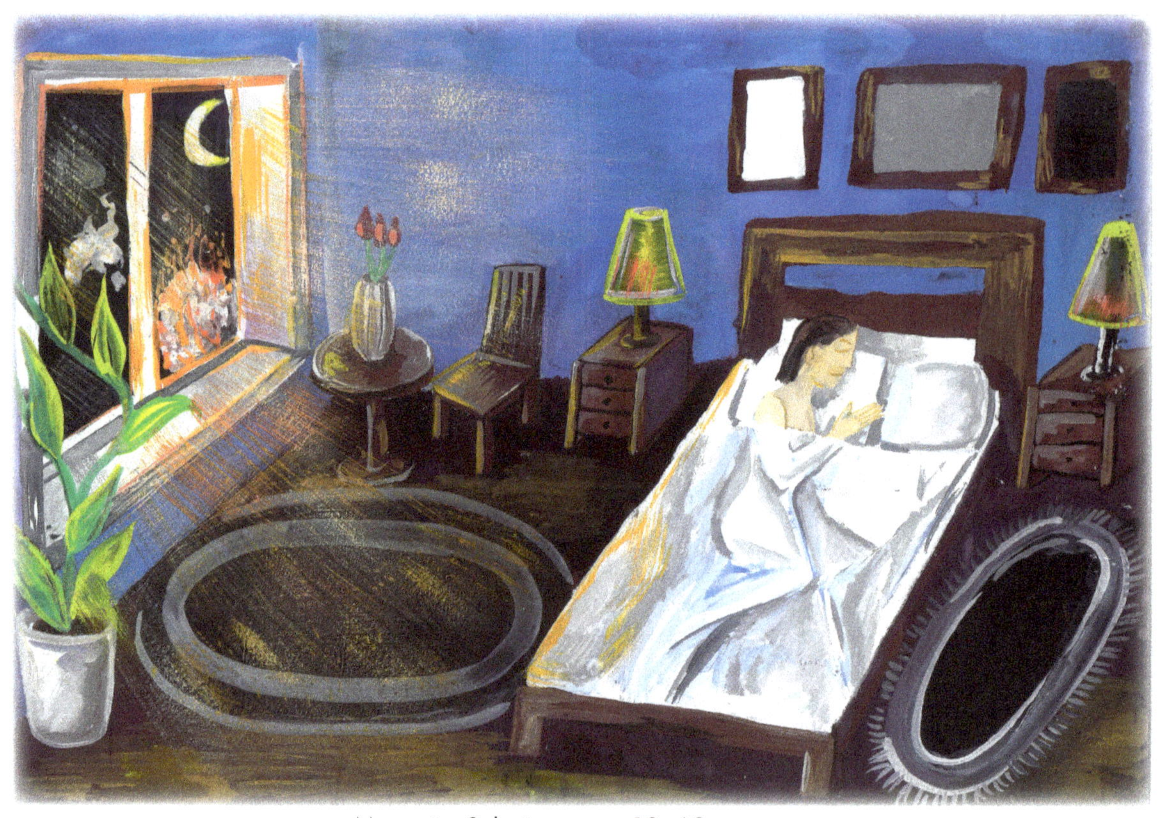

Margarita Soloviova, age 13, A3 tempera

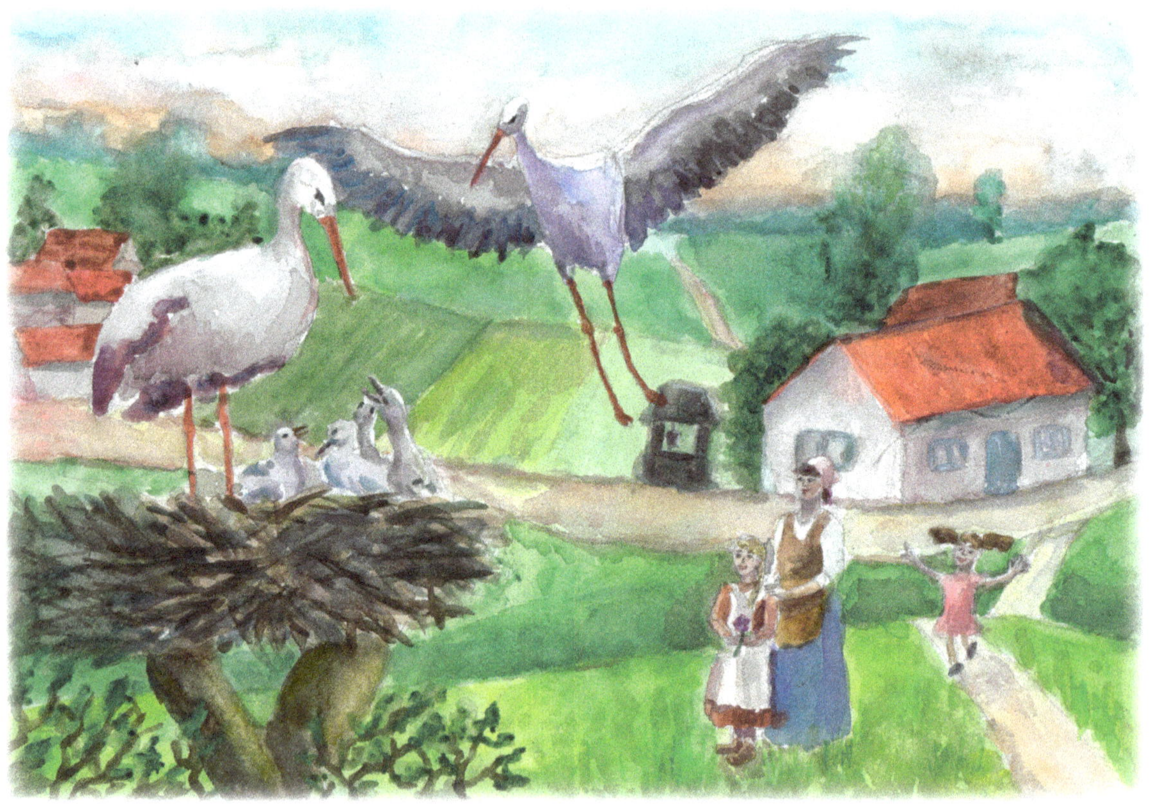

Valeriya Gluschenko, age 18, A3 watercolor

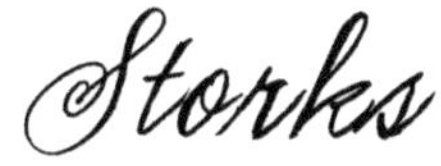

Storks

by Zhurba Kseniya, Ukraine

Late one night, on the 19th of April 2014, in a rural Ukrainian village, a loud sound woke Oksana up in the middle of the night. "Could it be Easter fireworks?" she wondered. Easter Sunday was the brightest and happiest holiday for her.

But these weren't fireworks; this was war. Volleys of automatic gunfire, grenades and explosions made her heart pound. Was this real? She went to the church and prayed. She could not have imagined the suffering ahead.

An artillery shell fell in their own garden. Fear filled her stomach. She found her daughters and hugged them for a long time as she cried.

She couldn't remember if the rain had ever made people so happy, but the shooting stopped when it rained. And that was enough.

For their children's safety, they decided to leave. But how to pack for the trip? They needed documents, money, and clothes. And what about the library of books collected over generations, the family photograph albums and her grandmother's icons, including a huge one she had inherited from her uncle? They would not fit in the bags. She cried. She went to the garden and took pictures of every shrub, tree, and flower. At least she would keep the memories.

"Mom," she said to her mother-in-law, "We're leaving tomorrow. Have you packed?"

"I'm not going. My life, my home, my husband's grave are all in this village. Who will take care of them if I'm gone? I was born here and I will die here. You go. Take my granddaughters to peace, quiet, and happiness. Your whole lives are before you."

They could not leave her. So, they stayed!

Once they decided to stay, Oksana's whole view of the world changed. Their problems united them with their neighbours. They supported each other. When the electricity went out for forty days, her husband and his friends found a generator, repaired it, and found fuel. In the evenings, everyone came to their house to charge their batteries. People shared food. In the evening they took buckets of milk from the cows in the village to the street. Children, adults, and even cats and dogs drank as much milk as they wanted.

Before then, they used to spend their evenings in front of the TV or the computer. Now they sat in the street and talked and exchanged advice. They figured out how to help each other clean a well. They organized water delivery to the elderly. They found medicines for people in need.

A pair of storks stayed in the village, too. People say they bring good luck. But to Oksana they brought joy. Despite the scorching summer heat, the storks hatched five chicks. They were not afraid of gunfire. They did not abandon their nest, they stayed and survived, just like the people of the village. In the autumn, the storks left… but can you believe it? They came back the next spring!

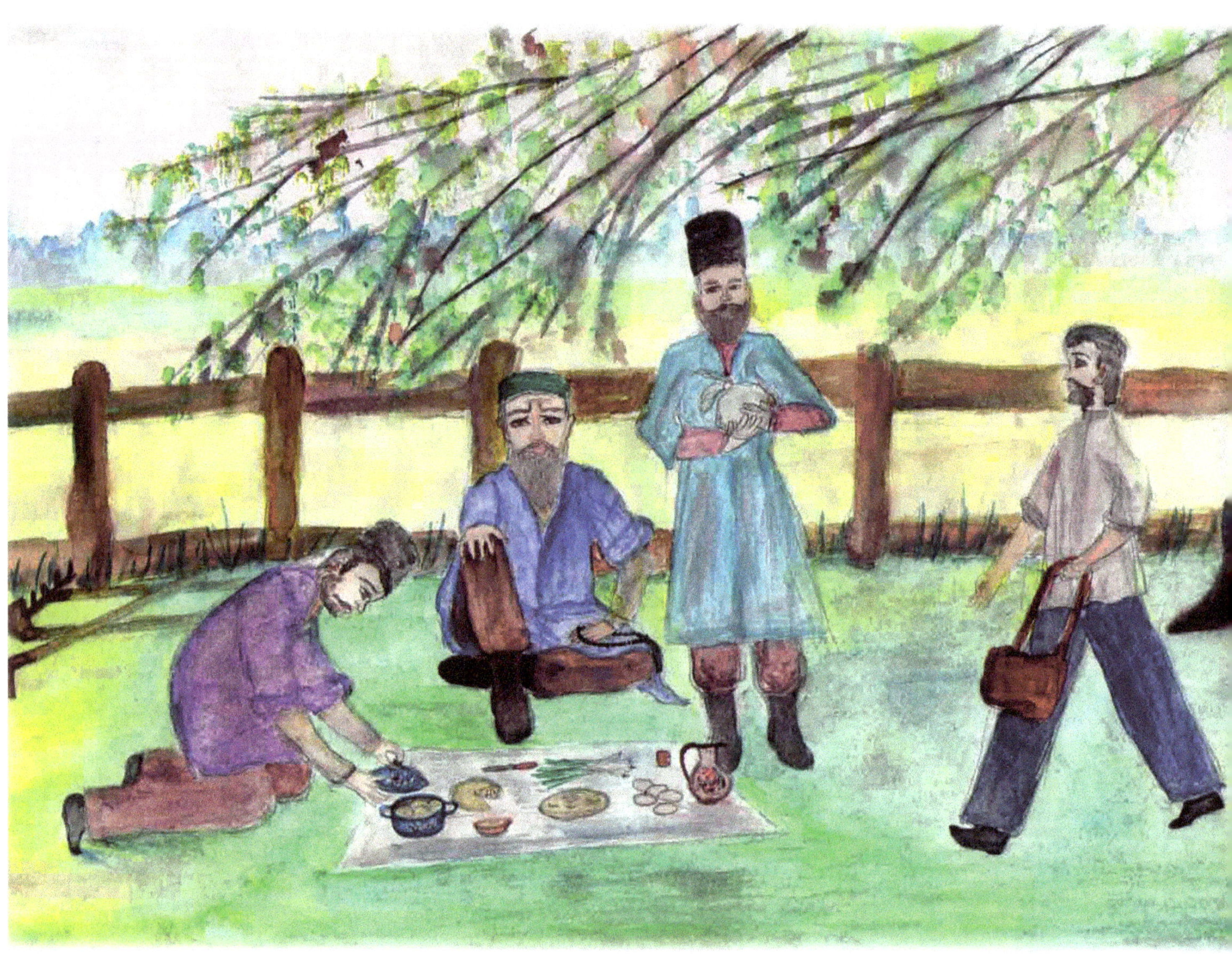

Unknown, 11.5 x 8 in. watercolor

Weeding the Field

by Musa Akhmadov, Chechnya

One day several Muslim students, known as *murid* in Chechen, agreed to help weed Kunta-hadji's maize field. They did not tell their spiritual teacher, *Ustaz* in Chechen, for they knew his temperament well. Instead they waited and when he went away they set off to the field, which lay along the edge of the forest.

This happened at the beginning of summer. Dewdrops hung on the grass and leaves sparkled in the rising sun. A chorus of birds could be heard, and crickets sang in the grass, as if in competition.

The *murid* sang their own songs while weeding. They worked quickly, soon clearing a wide strip of land. As if awakened, the shoots of maize seemed to stretch towards the sun, swaying in the gentle breeze. The *murid* were pleased. They rested awhile, then set to work again. But Kunta-hadji came to see what they were doing. They stopped work and greeted him.

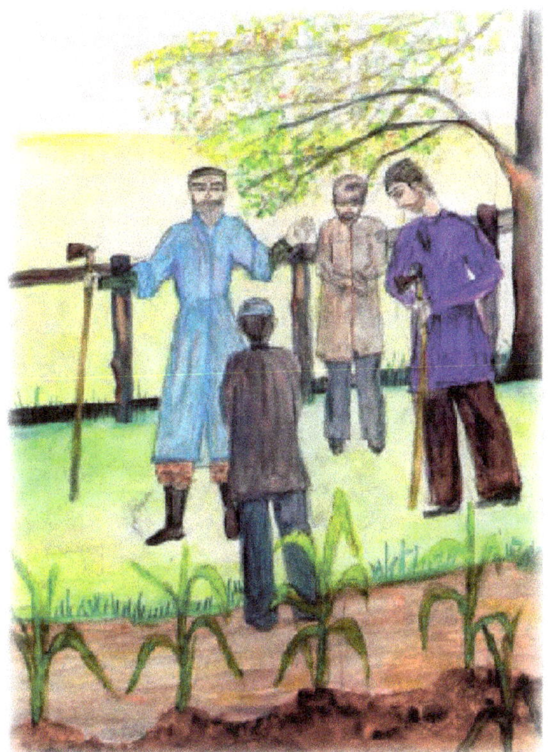

Unknown, lost original, watercolor

"What are you doing? Who told you to weed in my field?" Kunta-hadji asked.

The *murid* answered, "Nobody. We came because we wanted to help you."

"I can still do the weeding myself. If not, I would ask for your help. Now pick up your hoes and come here. All the maize in the part of the field you've weeded will belong to you. In autumn, come get it." Kunta-hadji sounded displeased and upset. The *murid* obeyed without protest, but felt hurt because he refused their help.

He sat down in the shade and called them to gather round. "Don't be angry. I made a vow in the name of Allah that I would use only what I gain by my own labour. Please forgive me if I caused you any hurt."

The students' eyes filled with tears. They replied, "How can we forgive you? Please forgive us for coming onto your field without your knowledge."

"Allah forgives you, as I do! Now let's spend some time together. We can try my maize bread, and talk things over." Kunta-hadji opened his knapsack, produced folded napkins, and offered them maize-bread and cheese. The *murid* offered what they had as well.

Time passed in eating and chatting about what had happened until the hour of the noon-tide prayer. They performed the rite with great devotion. Before they left for home, one of the *murid* made a request of their *Ustaz*, "Instruct us, please. Give us counsel."

Kunta-hadji answered, "I will speak of four things. Two you must forget, and the others you must constantly remember. Forget acts of kindness you can do for others. If you speak of them in public, Allah will give you no reward. Forget evil others do to you. By forgetting, you will forsake it, and it will forsake you. But never forget that we must die, and that we must appear before Allah."